DATE DUE			

The Political Economy
of Prosperity

The substance of this book
was presented as the Crawley Memorial Lectures
at the Wharton School of Finance and Commerce
of the University of Pennsylvania
in April 1969.

Arthur M. Okun

The Political Economy
of Prosperity

The Brookings Institution

WASHINGTON, D.C.

338.973

Or 7 p

75887

THE BROOKINGS INSTITUTION is an independent organization devoted to nonpartisan research, education, and publication in economics, government, foreign policy, and the social sciences generally. Its principal purposes are to aid in the development of sound public policies and to promote public understanding of issues of national importance.

The Institution was founded on December 8, 1927, to merge the activities of the Institute for Government Research, founded in 1916, the Institute of Economics, founded in 1922, and the Robert Brookings Graduate School of Economics and Government, founded in 1924.

The general administration of the Institution is the responsibility of a self-perpetuating Board of Trustees. The trustees are likewise charged with maintaining the independence of the staff and fostering the most favorable conditions for creative research and education. The immediate direction of the policies, program, and staff of the Institution is vested in the President, assisted by an advisory council chosen from the staff of the Institution.

In publishing a study, the Institution presents it as a competent treatment of a subject worthy of public consideration. The interpretations and conclusions in such publications are those of the author or authors and do not purport to represent the views of the other staff members, officers, or trustees of the Brookings Institution.

foreword

The decade of the 1960s witnessed remarkable developments in the performance of the U.S. economy. Contrary to many forecasts and fears expressed early in the decade, the vitality of the economy was emphatically demonstrated. It was a period of sustained growth, high employment, and brisk investment—unmarred by recession for almost nine years. But the record also shows a number of blemishes that now loom as major challenges for the 1970s. Prosperity was not accompanied by price stability, and inflation became more serious than at any time since 1951. Inflationary pressures placed heavy burdens on some private citizens, on some sectors of the industrial economy, and on financial markets.

These developments were accompanied by a greatly increased interest in economic policy and the overall performance of the economy. The public and the press became more familiar with the basic ideas and methods of economics. At the same time, professional economists played an increasingly important role in the political process.

Underlying these trends are the issues considered in this book. Some of them are questions of economic behavior—of the responses of consumers and businessmen to changes in fiscal and monetary policy and of wages and prices to shifts in the level of economic activity. Other questions concern the institutional framework for political decision making—the criteria by which policy makers formulate their choices, procedural arrangements that might help to avoid fiscal stalemates, and the appropriate exercise of federal influence on private wage and price decisions.

Still other issues test the social aims and public philosophy of the nation. They challenge its priorities and ask how it is possible to reconcile egalitarian principles with the persistence of poverty

v

amid abundance. But they also ask what are the proper limits on the federal government's power to determine economic policies.

These issues are the substance of political economy. Arthur M. Okun participated in many of the debates and innovations that characterized the political economy of the sixties. Now a Brookings Senior Fellow, he served for nearly six years as senior economist, then as a member, and finally as chairman of the President's Council of Economic Advisers. He devotes the first chapter to a consideration of the role of the professional economist in policy making, thus introducing the principal theme of the rest of the book: the problem of sustaining national prosperity.

Most of these ideas were presented in an earlier version as the Crawley Memorial Lectures at the Wharton School of Finance and Commerce of the University of Pennsylvania in the spring of 1969. In addition, a portion of Chapter 4 was presented as part of the Charles C. Moskowitz Lecture at New York University in November 1969. The author wishes to acknowledge the comments and criticisms of many friends and colleagues who read earlier drafts of the manuscript: Daniel Brill, William Capron, Samuel Chase, R. A. Gordon, Lawrence B. Krause, Wilfred Lewis, Jr., Edwin G. Nourse, Joseph A. Pechman, Merton J. Peck, George L. Perry, Walter Salant, Frank Schiff, Charles L. Schultze, Leonard S. Silk, and Charles B. Warden. Richard Morgenstern and William Rutledge assisted in the research; Evelyn Fisher contributed to the accuracy of facts and figures; Mary Green prepared the manuscript; Mendelle Berenson provided sympathetic editorial aid; and Helen Eisenhart prepared the index.

The views expressed in this book are the author's and do not necessarily reflect the views of the trustees, the officers, or other staff members of the Brookings Institution.

KERMIT GORDON
President

December 1969
Washington, D.C.

contents

chapter one

Consensus and Controversy in Political Economy

During the Kennedy and Johnson years, there was a major influx of economists into policy-level positions in the administration. Unlike most of their predecessors, the four Directors of the Bureau of the Budget and the two Under Secretaries of the Treasury for Monetary Affairs who served during the eight years were professional economists. Four new Governors of the Federal Reserve System—a majority of the Board—were chosen from the economics profession. The Pentagon civilian management was also invaded by economists. The Council of Economic Advisers (CEA) thus had much more company than in the past from their professional fraternity brothers.

Under the Nixon administration, it became clear that the phenomenon is bipartisan. The Bureau of the Budget remained the bailiwick of economists; the top management of Treasury became even more "economist," and the Pentagon continued to involve economists at high levels. A distinguished member of the profession was appointed to the newly created White House position of Counselor to the President; an outstanding academic labor economist was named Secretary of Labor. These presidential appointments are a ringing endorsement of the contribution that economists make in the policy process.

The changing of the guard in the executive branch underlines the agreements and the disagreements within the profession on public policy. Economists of contrasting political views agree among themselves on many issues. In particular, on a number of issues, a bipartisan majority of the profession would unite on the opposite side from a bipartisan majority of the Congress. However, areas of disagreement within the profession remain important and these are generally linked to differences in social

1

philosophy as well as differences in technical judgments about the workings of our economy. This chapter is devoted to a discussion of the scope and bases of professional consensus and of professional controversy on matters of economic policy.

The economist's influence is best known in the area of policy to influence overall business conditions. The tasks of promoting prosperity and avoiding recession, curbing inflation and achieving price stability—which are the main focus of the subsequent chapters—have long been recognized generally as the territory of the economist. However skeptical the public may be about the ability of economists to solve these problems, it does not know any group that is more reliable. The economist may not be believed or trusted, but he will not be ignored. When called upon to make a major tax decision, every elected federal official— from the President to a freshman member of the House of Representatives—knows that he is traveling on economic terrain and does not need to be reminded to seek the views of economists. He will surely also want to hear opinions from others—especially from the leaders of business and labor. But even these views will be influenced by the economists who advise the leaders of the private economy.

The influence of the economist on policy, however, is not limited to clearly defined *economic* programs and problems. The political decision maker faces thousands of problems which are primarily social or national security or international or racial issues. Yet almost every problem and proposed solution has an economic side, involving material benefits and costs and affecting the use of manpower and capital. One of the major responsibilities of economists in central positions—like the Bureau of the Budget or the Council of Economic Advisers— is to ensure that the economic aspects of such decisions will not be ignored. In many cases, they can demonstrate that alternative programs, equally capable of fulfilling a national security or social objective, deserve widely different grades for economic consequences.

To take one example of relevance in recent years, proposals to reduce pollution surely do not come to the President as *economic* policy. Yet pollution policy has been an area of intensive staff work by economists. This interest was reflected in the 1966 Annual Report of the Council in a small section headed "Rubbish, Garbage, and Junk Automobiles." [1] (Some readers have long felt that the Council's Reports were full of rubbish, garbage, and junk, but this was the first time that the CEA agreed.) More generally, as Charles Schultze has recently discussed in detail, the planning, programming, and budgeting system adopted by the federal government for all agencies in 1965 is developing into a comprehensive and concerted effort to apply the economic yardstick to the many choices in the federal budget.[2]

The Economist's Approach

Obviously economists are individuals with diverse talents and aptitudes: Some are good speech writers; some are imaginative creators of programs and projects; others are excellent salesmen of ideas; a few even turn out by luck to be good administrators. Nevertheless, economists tend to share some common ways of thinking, resulting largely from the training program that our universities give to young people who subsequently are called economists. The program is designed to give the student a particular way of viewing problems and particular skills in solving them; to some extent, it succeeds.

Whatever the problem set before the economist, his technique in solving it reflects his training. The analytical approach to choice is the hallmark of the profession. It is the essence of the discipline to focus on, and especially to quantify, the dimensions of choice—the costs, the benefits, and the alternative ways to achieve a given result. Most of what we know professionally about the process of analyzing choices is surprisingly simple and

1. *Economic Report of the President together with the Annual Report of the Council of Economic Advisers, January 1966*, p. 123.
2. Charles L. Schultze, *The Politics and Economics of Public Spending* (Brookings Institution, 1968).

yet astonishingly useful; apparently the simple truths are not always learned in the school of hard knocks or the temple of common sense.

First, the economist looks for the opportunities sacrificed in selecting any alternative; he is professionally qualified to apply thoroughly and unrelentingly the propositions that you can't get something for nothing and that you can't have your cake and eat it too. Whether some specific federal action is a good thing can be decided only in terms of what the nation has to forgo in order to make the endeavor possible. Every proposal aims to further some worthy objective. A meaningful evaluation requires a careful analysis of what other objectives it may impede either directly, or indirectly by using up resources that could go elsewhere.

Second, the economist recognizes that the closest one ever comes to getting something for nothing is by increasing efficiency and productivity. Where that is possible, more can be obtained in one area without sacrificing and taking less in others. The potential for improvement in productivity and efficiency is the great reconciler in economic policies.

Third, the economist takes a marginalist or incremental approach by asking how much *extra* is obtained by doing something *extra*. "What difference does it make?" is the key question. By keeping his eye on this ball, the economist can ensure against post hoc, propter hoc reasoning. The empirical verification and quantification of marginal effects of policy actions are exceedingly challenging. They are the core of the research about economic behavior that is most relevant to policy.

The wise economist knows, however, that merely finding a marginal-this to be compared with a marginal-that is not sufficient for an evaluation. A rigidly incrementalist approach can lose sight of major opportunities. Locating the least soggy spot in a swamp is not optimizing if high ground is accessible outside the swamp. The fruitful applications of global "systems analysis" demonstrate that economists need not succumb to marginalist myopia. Moreover, the economist is trained to recognize the time dimension of the effects that he appraises. Short-run and long-run consequences of programs differ, and the analyst looks beyond immediate results to subsequent repercussions and ramifications.

Fourth, the economist recognizes the diverse uses of resources and the opportunities for substitution among them. These principles often lead to a preference ˙ for seemingly roundabout or indirect solutions. The employment problems of textile workers in New England cities may be solved by the development of an electronics industry. A tax cut can create jobs for the poor even though they benefit little directly from lower tax bills.

Because money is fungible—capable of being divided and shifted around—the direct approach that strikes the politician's fancy may not work. It often *seems* most effective to support an earmarked purpose by such direct means as a grant to a locality for education, a tax incentive to a businessman for manpower training, or a gift of food to a less developed country. But it may be virtually impossible to assure that such measures really hit their target. The recipient can respond by spending less of his own funds on the stated objective and more elsewhere, thus turning the aid into a general purpose grant. Hence roundabout routes may be more effective, even if they appear paradoxical to the layman. The man in the street knows that the penicillin designed to cure his sore throat is not injected into his throat; but he does not have similar experience with the flow of economic medicine through the body politic.

Fifth, the economist trained in the Anglo-Saxon tradition has a predisposition to believe that the best way to serve the interest of a rational, well-informed adult is to let him make his own choices insofar as they do not conflict with the welfare of others.

Finally, the economist sees the competitive market and its pricing mechanism as a particularly efficient way of giving expression to individual choices and of reconciling private and public interests.

It is remarkable how many of the campaigns, crusades, and battles of economists in public service are predicated in one way or another on these simple propositions. They are the foundation for a considerable area of agreement within the profession. It is news when economists disagree, but the broad range of agreement among professionals of differing political philosophies often goes unnoticed. In particular, there is widespread professional agreement about things the government should *not* do, what Charles Hitch once called the profession's "non-agenda of government." [3]

An economist interested in public policy is likely to be a free trader. He can demonstrate analytically that, under a broad set of conditions, barriers to the international exchange of goods and services induce a net reduction in worldwide efficiency. He will, of course, recognize exceptions to this rule as well as other cases where, even though the world economy loses, our own nation may come out ahead. But, when he umpires, any protectionist proposal comes up to bat with at least one strike against it.

In domestic areas as well, the economist is likely to be skeptical of proposals that would stifle the price mechanism, whether by setting ceilings or floors on prices or by restraining competitive behavior. Whatever the ideological stripe of an administration or congressional body, its economists are likely to be among those least enthusiastic about agricultural programs based on contrived scarcity, ceilings on interest rates, rapid advances in the minimum wage, floors on rates in transportation industries, resale price maintenance (so-called fair trade agreements), and other controls and constraints on prices or wages. Free choice and competition expressed through purchasing and selling decisions of individual competitors often have a remarkable property of yielding social results that cannot be improved on by public action. At the same time, the market has many defects and shortcomings that require public action. In dealing with these defects, the economist is happiest when he can recommend a public policy that works to perfect the market rather than to overrule or finesse it.

3. Charles J. Hitch, "The Uses of Economics," in Pendleton Herring, Philip E. Mosely, Charles J. Hitch, and others, *Research for Public Policy* (Brookings Institution, 1961), p. 96.

The Economist versus the Special Interest

If economists who vote Democratic and economists who vote Republican are united on many issues in their field of professional expertise, then why are their agreements not always reflected in the law of the land? One answer emerges from a simple review of the programs on which I have suggested that present statutes and professional consensus are at variance. Whatever the economics profession may think about agricultural price supports, high barriers against oil imports, or minimum rates in transportation, some groups in our nation have an obvious stake in these measures. Many of the interest groups in our society want a shield against the market, and some have the political influence and power to get one. Generally these are likely to be producers' groups, and the economist is often cast in the role of the consumer's champion.

In some cases, the producer's interest coincides with, or is consistent with, the public interest. The producer's claim to special treatment may reflect a legitimate gripe or bring to light an imperfection in the workings of the system. Our pluralistic political process relies upon individuals and groups to present their views and press their cases. Ungreased wheels are expected to squeak for themselves.

Yet the producer's interest diverges from the public interest in many areas; such cases have been recognized and amply documented in the literature of economics from Adam Smith to Henry Simons.[4] And the literature of my profession, as well as that of political science, records the potency of special interests. Still it comes as a surprise and disappointment to the novice in Washington to learn just how much such groups influence the legislative process.

The strong and concerted wishes of the few tend to get dis-

4. Adam Smith, *An Inquiry into the Nature and Causes of the Wealth of Nations* (London: 3rd ed., Methuen, 1922), Vol. 1, esp. Chap. 10, "Of Wages and Profit in the Different Employments of Labour and Stock"; Henry C. Simons, *Economic Policy for a Free Society* (University of Chicago Press, 1948), esp. Chap. 2, "A Positive Program for Laissez Faire: Some Proposals for a Liberal Economic Policy."

proportional weight relative to the weak and diffused interests of the many. The key is not primarily wealth or class; small businessmen and farmers are as powerful in this respect as the mighty giants of the petroleum industry. It takes a well-organized, unified minority willing to put on the line its political support, its votes, and its efforts on the basis of a single group of issues. Thus dairy import quotas involve bread as well as butter to a couple of hundred thousand dairy farmers; they mean at most a few cents a day to a couple of hundred million other Americans. The dairy farmers will know and remember how their congressmen vote on this issue; the housewife will almost certainly either ignore or forget it, and her husband surely will. Political realities impel a congressman to tax the majority of his constituency lightly in order to benefit a small interest group heavily.

Economists in government spend much time and energy rebutting the claims of special interest groups. They have to shoot down repeatedly the lengthy briefs prepared by the economists in the employ of such groups, who eagerly invoke the support and defense of economic arguments to claim that their interest really does coincide with the public interest. The economist in the public service always faces the threat that bad economics will drive out good. And he has to run fast just to avoid losing ground.

In fact, we have run at least fast enough to hold our own in the sixties. Special interest groups have not made new and greater inroads in the law. We can even point to a few areas of progress. American trade policy became freer under Presidents Kennedy and Johnson. President Johnson viewed liberal trade as a fundamental principle and was willing to fight for it. Once, for example, when presented privately with a proposal that was billed as "only a little protectionist," he squashed it with the retort that it reminded him of the girl who was only a little bit pregnant. Also, in the Johnson years, the consumer was provided with a network of safeguards against deceitful and harmful practices, lack of information, and misinformation that impair his free choice in the market.

Finally, the balance of political power was improved by interest groups formed in areas of new government initiative. Organized political expression by the poor and lobbying by educators and even by operators of nursing homes followed the initiation of government programs; these offset some of the power of more traditional special interests. Although the new lobbies could prove troublesome in the future, their interests were generally in tune with national priorities during the sixties.

There have, however, been many instances of frustration and defeat. President Kennedy's program for deregulation of transportation was stillborn in 1962. The response to the 1963 Kennedy initiative for tax reform was most discouraging. After years of internal work to devise a maritime program that might have some chance of enactment, President Johnson's proposals did not gain an inch in the legislative process. Congress failed regularly to act on presidential proposals for more reliance on user charges for federal facilities. On one occasion President Johnson authorized Gardner Ackley and me to get the reaction of some congressional leaders to the Council's argument in favor of repeal of fair trade laws. The first thing that caught my eye in one office was a plaque recording the appreciation of a retailers' trade association for the achievements of that congressman. We did not get an enthusiastic reception.

Given the strength and the bitterness of the opposition, a presidential crusade against shields and subsidies seemed most unpromising. Particularly in the early 1960s, far greater gains were to be made by fighting to enlarge the size of the national economic pie than by pressing proposals to increase equity and efficiency in sharing the pie. Improved overall performance of the national economy could be legitimately sold as good for everybody, and thus fitted into the Johnsonian consensus approach. Where redistribution was at issue, it seemed most important to focus on political power by enhancing the strength of the weak and the disadvantaged at the ballot box and in community decision making. Thus for understandable—though regrettable—reasons, the shields and subsidies continue on the statute books into the seventies.

Efficiency and Equity

The cases where the professional verdict is overruled by the minority can be readily documented and lamented. But there are also many cases in which the economist's answer conflicts with the views of the majority. Often the divergence arises out of public misunderstanding, which then requires mass education in elementary economics. This was particularly important in regard to the tax proposals of 1963 and 1967, which I shall discuss in Chapters 2 and 3.

In other cases, however, the economist's judgments about efficiency are rejected because they do not accord with the public's concept of equity. The structure of welfare economics rests on what economists call the "Pareto condition": A measure improves social efficiency if its benefits *exceed* what is required to compensate fully everyone whose welfare is impaired. In fact, the people harmed normally are not compensated and this is a basis for legitimate concern. A democratic capitalism must perform a perpetual juggling act to keep the balance between equity and efficiency. In a society with egalitarian principles, substantial inequality in income and wealth is tolerated only as a concession to efficiency. The inequality arises through the carrots and sticks of a market system. Sometimes the carrots are awarded to the wise, the energetic, and the ingenious; such results square with society's sense of fair play. Even the working of the stick may be supported when it falls on the foolish and the lazy.

In many instances, however, rewards and penalties are not neatly equated with personal merit. Any economics textbook describes some results which are generated by a blind lottery rather than a wise jury. If consumer demand shifts from hats to shoes, then shoe producers are rewarded with greater profits and hat producers are penalized with lower incomes. This redistribution has the socially desirable consequence of encouraging investment and employment in the production of shoes and of discouraging expansion in the hat industry. But the public cannot applaud when some able and honest businessmen fail and some efficient and energetic workers become unemployed. Nor does the nation cheer when some citizens just happen to have the pot of gold land in their laps.

The market generates a distribution of income which is a by-product of its solution of the problems of allocation and production. The solutions to these problems have certain demonstrably ideal properties, but the resulting income distribution has no inherent logic.

It is quite understandable that the distribution result is sometimes deplored by the majority. Some economists who have advised less developed countries report widespread opposition to the allocation of food by market-clearing prices. Cumbersome and inefficient rationing systems are actually preferred. In the view of the public, it is bad enough that food is scarce; it would be unconscionable for food to be expensive too. Support for rent ceilings in this country is analogous: People want to prevent rich landlords from gouging poor tenants. But rent controls destroy incentives to maintain or rehabilitate property, and are thus an assured way to preserve slums. (When I read that some Harvard students were actively campaigning for rent ceilings in Cambridge and Boston, I wondered how many of that group were economics majors.)

The public is usually hostile to the proposal frequently made by economists for charging premium rates on subways, buses, or bridges at peak hours.[5] Here justice seems to be violated because the peak-hour traveler gets the worst service—most crowding, slowest ride, and so forth. If he had any options or a high enough income, he would not be one of the sardines. How can he decently be charged an *extra* fee compared with those who travel in leisurely luxury during slack hours?

These attitudes are not entirely unreasonable and they cannot be dismissed. The economist is challenged to find solutions

5. See, for example, William S. Vickrey, "Pricing in Urban and Suburban Transport," in American Economic Association, *Papers and Proceedings of the Seventy-fifth Annual Meeting, 1962* (*American Economic Review,* Vol. 53, May 1963), pp. 452–65.

which preserve efficiency and still meet public standards of equity. He is also challenged to educate the public on the importance of the efficiency criteria he applies. The economist's job is to enlighten democratic decisions—not to attempt to impose technocratic decisions in the policy process.

With a little ingenuity, economists frequently can devise solutions that reconcile efficiency with the democratic notion of equity. This is particularly true in meeting the burdens of transition which so often concern the nation. When workers or firms are displaced by technological advance, aids to relocation and retraining deserve more stress. Adjustment assistance offers a particularly promising approach to ameliorate the impact of shifts in international trade. When businessmen and workers are severely injured by changing patterns of imports, they can be given temporary aid in shifting to other productive efforts. This means of cushioning the blow need not detract from the efficiency of the national economy and can be far less costly to the nation than the perpetuation of barriers to broader trade with other countries.

The Negative Income Tax

Taxation is a key to linking equity and efficiency. The progressive income tax—despite all the current defects and limitations of our tax laws—is our most important and most efficient means of modifying the upper end of the income distribution. There is a growing—although far from complete—professional consensus [6] in favor of extending the same principle to the low end of the income scale through a negative income tax, which would establish a guaranteed income floor and would provide

6. See, for example, Milton Friedman, *Capitalism and Freedom* (University of Chicago Press, 1962), esp. pp. 190–95; Christopher Green, *Negative Taxes and the Poverty Problem* (Brookings Institution, 1967); Robert Theobald (ed.), *The Guaranteed Income: Next Step in Economic Evolution?* (Doubleday, 1966); James Tobin, Joseph A. Pechman, and Peter M. Mieszkowski, "Is a Negative Income Tax Practical?" *Yale Law Journal*, Vol. 77 (November 1967), pp. 1–27 (Brookings Reprint 142).

for a sliding scale of payments diminishing with rises in a family's earnings. The best way for the poor to raise their incomes is, of course, through improved opportunities for gainful employment. More and better jobs for the poor have indeed been the main escape route out of poverty during the sixties. But because of this very progress, relatively more of the poor are now in groups that, because of age, disability, or family situation, are least likely to achieve satisfactory opportunities for work. For these groups, cash benefits are the main hope for raising living standards. While there is a rationale for specific programs of in-kind benefits in the form of food, rent, or medicine, most economists regard the malnutrition, inadequate housing, and poor health of the poor primarily as symptoms of their inadequate income rather than as separate problems to be attacked by different routes. An economist on the CEA staff once offered a typical professional reaction when, after reviewing a host of in-kind proposals, he expressed the hope that money might soon be invented in our society.

Of course, cash benefits are offered to those among the poor who are classified as eligible for welfare. But the eligibility standards reflect an effort to distinguish between the "deserving" and "undeserving" poor—a distinction that defies justification on either philosophical or economic grounds. In practice, the efforts to retain penalties on the "undeserving" adult poor often condemn their children to a life of poverty. As a supplement to other necessary and desirable efforts, a program of guaranteed income could greatly increase the logic and efficiency of public aid to the poor. To be sure, steps would be required to assure that work incentives are maintained. The poor will not work for no added income any more than the rich. But we deal quite effectively with this problem at the upper end of the income scale. Just as the present income tax does not seriously impede incentives to earn high incomes, the negative income tax need not interfere significantly with incentives to augment low incomes.

The negative income tax looks like a "right answer" to a difficult question. Yet public opinion polls record the overwhelming opposition of the American public to any system of guaranteed income that does not depend directly on work efforts. In June 1968, for example, the Gallup Poll found that more than 80 percent of those expressing an opinion favored a plan that provided for an above-poverty income through guaranteed employment opportunity, but more than 60 percent opposed the income floor without a work requirement.[7] These expressions of public opinion suggest that it would be very difficult to enact a full-dress negative income tax under present circumstances. Moreover, they warn us that, even if the negative income tax could be enacted, it might become an instrument of social divisiveness. It might generate a wave of resentment by the middle class and a strong feeling of being demeaned on the part of the recipients. Before economists can conclude that we have the "right answer" in this area, we have to understand and educate the American public. For one thing, it is doubtful that the public realizes how many of the poor are unable to work, by any reasonable standard.

The family assistance program proposed by President Nixon in the summer of 1969 is a major step toward the negative income tax for families with children.[8] It may well be as large a step as our society will accept at this time. The plan effectively eliminates the categories of eligibility for public assistance and hence terminates the pointless distinction between the deserving and undeserving poor. One vestige of this distinction, however, remains in the form of a requirement that recipients of this assistance be prepared to accept "suitable jobs." Given the modest level of the federal payment—$1,600 a year for a family of four—and the 50 percent net retention of earned income, I strongly doubt that the work requirement is seriously needed. Moreover, it would be enforceable only through a

7. *New York Times,* June 16, 1968.

8. Immediately after President Nixon set forth his welfare proposals in August 1969, the Gallup Poll found overwhelming public support for them. See "The President's Address to the Nation on Domestic Programs," *Weekly Compilation of Presidential Documents,* Vol. 5 (Aug. 11, 1969), pp. 1103–12; and *New York Times,* Aug. 31, 1969.

revival of strict categorical definitions in a new guise, which might nullify the progress offered by this program. I would expect good sense to triumph in limiting enforcement to the rare flagrant cases of freeloading. Apparently, some statutory antilaziness requirement is a political imperative for the program. In the days of temperance laws it was sometimes said that the most viable social compromise required that the "drys" get their laws while the "wets" get their liquor. Perhaps, at this juncture in society, the reactionaries must get their work provision when the poor get their aid.

International Exchange Rates

In another important area—international exchange rates— the profession has a "right answer" which is only gradually winning acceptance among bankers, businessmen, and statesmen.

Research economists and academic experts today agree broadly, although not unanimously, that a greater degree of flexibility in exchange rates would be a desirable innovation.[9] Under the present system of pegged exchange rates, changes in relative currency values are difficult to accomplish, so that nations get locked into valuations which are inconsistent with their domestic stabilization objectives. To reconcile the irreconcilable, they often turn to measures which raise barriers to the international flow of goods and capital. Moreover, as a set of administered prices, the pegged exchange system does not pro-

9. See, for example, Milton Friedman, "First Lecture," in Milton Friedman and Robert V. Roosa, *The Balance of Payments: Free Versus Fixed Exchange Rate*s (Washington: American Enterprise Institute for Public Policy Research, 1967), pp. 1–24; George N. Halm, *Toward Limited Exchange-Rate Flexibility* (Princeton University, Department of Economics, International Finance Section, 1969); James E. Meade, "The Case for Variable Exchange Rates," in Warren L. Smith and Ronald L. Teigen (eds.), *Readings in Money, National Income and Stabilization Policy* (Richard D. Irwin, 1965), pp. 505–17. For an opposing expert view, see Charles P. Kindleberger, "The Case for Fixed Exchange Rates, 1969" (paper presented at the Bald Peak Monetary Conference, sponsored by the Federal Reserve Bank of Boston, Melvin Village, N.H., Oct. 9, 1969).

vide the flexibility and the opportunities for gradual adjustment
and for economizing that would exist under market-determined
exchange rates. If marks are scarce relative to francs, the whole
philosophy of a market mechanism argues that the relative
prices of the two currencies ought to adjust accordingly. But
this prescription, broadly accepted by professional economic
experts, is still acceptable to only a minority of international
traders and investors and dealers in world exchange markets.

Most practitioners in the world economy see flexibility of
exchange rates as an additional source of risk and uncertainty.[10]
The exponent of greater flexibility can point out that, under
the system of pegged rates, the relative exchange rate between
francs and marks has been highly uncertain at times, and that
the major revaluations which occur infrequently can be far
more disruptive than gradual adjustments over time. He can
also argue that the initiation of greater flexibility in exchange
rates would promote the development of better markets offering insurance and hedging opportunities to those who need
protection against future changes in exchange rates. He can
finally point to commercial, financial, and political uncertainties that simply swamp the exchange rate uncertainty in their
impact on world commercial and financial transactions.

Still the doubts and reservations of the skeptics persist. In
particular, they can document a generation of unparalleled success in the liberalization and growth of world trade and world
capital movements. They can stress the risk of disrupting a
system that has been a consistent winner: Why throw in a pat
hand? The repeated signs of crisis so evident in the last few
years argue for timely preventive action to modify the existing
system while it is still a winner. Along with most of my professional colleagues, I believe we must travel the road toward
greater flexibility. But more flexible rates will become a correct
and feasible answer only when they are better understood by
the world financial community. If introduced today, flexible

10. See "O'Brien Rejects Floating Rates," *London Financial Times,*
Sept. 17, 1969.

rates might have disruptive results in the short run. Because traders and investors might be frightened away from some international activities, the new system might impose unacceptable transition costs and indeed conceivably might not survive its initiation period.

To make a more flexible system economically reliable as well as politically feasible, intensive education is necessary. In order to convince those affected that legitimate interests can and will be protected, economists must learn to understand the precise character of the concerns and anxieties that international businessmen and bankers feel about greater flexibility. Education has to proceed in both directions. The exchange trader can help to teach the economist how greater flexibility can be tailored to the needs of the currency markets. The economist's basic objective of greater flexibility can be achieved by a number of alternative techniques and the practitioners have much to contribute in drawing up the specific blueprint.

The educational process is developing in encouraging ways. Some outstanding international economists who are exponents of greater flexibility have been discussing the issues with international bankers and traders in meetings of the new Conference on Proposals for Greater Flexibility of Exchange Rates.[11] This is proving to be a flexible exchange of views.

What Consensus?

Our ability as economists to influence public policy in the areas of professional agreement is impaired by the difficulty of establishing the existence of consensus. In fact, nobody really knows how to define or measure a consensus, and I could be challenged on a number of areas where I have claimed that the profession is generally agreed.

11. The Conference was organized by Robert V. Roosa, Fritz Machlup, and George N. Halm. The first meeting was held Jan. 29–31, 1969, at Oyster Bay, N.Y.; subsequent meetings have been at Burgenstock, Switzerland, June 23–29, 1969, and at the Brookings Institution, Oct. 1, 1969.

The economics profession is richly endowed with thousands of qualified experts and, on almost any particular issue, at least a few hundred are likely to differ honestly with the rest of their colleagues. The view of a small minority will get considerable attention in the press just because of its novelty. And when the Congress is looking for the testimony of experts, it makes every effort to select a balanced panel so that both sides can be heard. The staff of one congressional committee had a particularly difficult assignment when, in 1968, it was forced to beat the bushes to find some "respectable" expert who would testify *against* Special Drawing Rights—the widely supported plan for augmenting international liquidity with fiat money.

The existence of a professional consensus in favor of a tax increase in the fall of 1967 was reflected in a petition to the Congress bearing the signatures of 260 economists. Yet it was possible for Senator William Proxmire to state accurately that that list represented less than 2½ percent of the membership of the American Economic Association. In June 1969, a group of sixteen well-known economists covering the political spectrum made a similar plea for extension of the tax surcharge, relying on the prestige of the signatories rather than the count of noses.[12]

Some nations have formed duly constituted nonpartisan or bipartisan groups which can command respect as a kind of Supreme Court of economic advice. Examples are the Economic Council of Canada and the German Council of Experts.[13] But for reasons which I believe compelling, the U.S. Council of Economic Advisers functions in a much more controversial and partisan atmosphere, and makes no claim or attempt to act as a Supreme Court of economic views.

12. *Congressional Record,* Vol. 113, Pt. 19, 90 Cong. 1 sess. (1967), pp. 25063–65; *New York Times,* June 11, 1969.
13. For an interesting comparison of the German institution to the CEA, see Henry C. Wallich, "The American Council of Economic Advisers and the German Sachverstaendigenrat: A Study in the Economics of Advice," *Quarterly Journal of Economics,* Vol. 82 (August 1968), pp. 349–79.

Professional Controversy

The overriding objection to proposals that would focus the activities of the political economist on areas of consensus is precisely that they would remove him from the areas of controversy. They would limit him to the role of a pure technician. As technicians, economists are not pure; and we are more than technicians. Our philosophical and ideological positions are part of our professional views and our potential contribution.

One has to search hard for professional controversies—even on "purely" theoretical or empirical issues—that are independent of differing ideologies. The best example I can offer is the disagreement among students of business investment regarding the relative importance of internal cash flow, the cost of external capital, and the growth of final demand as determining factors. Even here, the accelerator school, which regards the growth of final demand as the key determinant of investment, seems to have no adherents who are politically conservative.

Most of the key policy controversies among economists reflect different philosophies about the government's role in the society and the economy, and about the relative priority attached to various objectives that we all value to some degree. There is no logical necessity for economists who place a particularly heavy weight on the goal of price stability also to favor a minimum size and scope of the federal budget, or to emphasize the importance of balance-of-payments equilibrium. Yet empirically this association exists. If you knew the views of an unidentified economist on half a dozen controversial issues, you could make a good estimate of his positions on six other issues.

In the areas of fiscal and monetary policy, economists sometimes disagree about the general ability of government to promote better economic performance by discretionary policy decisions. Those who advocate that monetary policy be guided by specific rules have a consistent ideological position reflecting their distrust of judgment and decision making in the bureaucratic process. Apart from this particular debate, the key to varying fiscal-monetary prescriptions lies in differing assessments of the relative social importance of price stability and of high employment. To be sure, the experts differ with one another at times on their forecasts of private demand and on their choice of stabilization instruments. Such differences in technical judgments can lead to occasional disagreements among people with the same philosophical orientation. Thus in some instances Walter Heller and Paul Samuelson disagree on the right prescription; and at times Arthur Burns and Henry Wallich disagree. And, on many occasions, all four agree.

But the ideological differences dominate the disagreements. There are "high-pressure" and "low-pressure" economists, to use Henry Wallich's apt term.[14] History probably does not record a day when Paul Samuelson was advocating restraint while Henry Wallich urged stimulus. When there are risks to be taken, Samuelson will accept a somewhat greater danger of inflation and Wallich will take somewhat more risk of unemployment. Price stability and high levels of employment are prized by both men, but not with the same relative intensity.

James Tobin has stated the high-pressure creed eloquently:

. . . The whole purpose of the economy is production of goods or services for consumption now or in the future. I think the burden of proof should always be on those who would produce less rather than more, on those who would leave idle men or machines or land that could be used. It is amazing how many reasons can be found to justify such waste: fears of inflation, balance-of-payments deficits, unbalanced budgets, excessive national debt, loss of confidence in the dollar. . . . Perhaps price stability, fixed exchange rates, balanced budgets, and the like can be justified as means to achieving and sustaining high employment, production, and consumption. Too often the means are accorded precedence over the end. . . .[15]

In the microeconomic area, sharp controversies arise among economists regarding the capability of political action to improve imperfect results of the market's decisions. The areas of consensus described above reflect a general commitment of

14. Henry C. Wallich, "Conservative Economic Policy," *Yale Review,* Vol. 46 (Autumn 1956), p. 68.

15. James Tobin, *National Economic Policy: Essays* (Yale University Press, 1966), pp. vii–viii.

economists to the impersonal and efficient solutions of the market mechanism in cases where competition prevails, where buyers and sellers are well informed, and where there are no externalities—that is, where benefits and costs are limited to consumers and producers of a given product. In such a world, the scope of microeconomic policy would be limited to modifying income distribution. But these assumptions are not a good description of the real world, and not a perfect description of any specific situation.

Any economist who wants the government to "do something about it" whenever the market falls short of perfection will prescribe an unlimited scope for government intervention. As George Stigler put it in a widely circulated comment, this prescription is like the verdict of the judge in a singing contest who was ready to award the prize to the second singer merely on the basis of having heard the first. The real question is whether any modification that could be introduced by government action would improve the situation.

On the other hand, conditions in the market sometimes fail to bear even a family resemblance to those of the model. Some situations virtually cry out for public intervention. For example, it is cold comfort that, without food and drug regulation, any customer who is fatally poisoned by a medication will never buy that product again. Political solutions can be workable and can improve matters on many occasions when the market solution is strongly tainted. And political action can bring the income distribution generated by the market closer into line with our egalitarian principles.

The microeconomic policies and programs of government aim to narrow the wide gap between the ideal world of the competitive model and the complex world we actually inhabit. Obviously, in many areas, the consumer does not receive adequate information to make intelligent choices without government safeguards and intervention. In some areas, economies of scale are so important that effective competition is impossible or woefully inefficient; hence the real choice is between regulated and unregulated monopoly. In such cases as pollution and neighborhood renewal, benefits and costs are not confined to the individual producer and the particular consumer; hence the decisions made by the parties directly involved in a transaction will neglect the interests of many others who have an important stake in the outcome.

Many goods—like national defense and lighthouses—simply cannot be provided by the market, and the government must shoulder the responsibility. Thus public policy aims to ensure competition whenever possible, to improvise substitutes for competition where it cannot work, to improve the flow of information, to supply services which are valued by the public collectively but which would not be adequately supplied in response to private market choice, and to reflect the social costs (and benefits) of production that are not borne (or captured) by the producer.

Health care is one of the many areas where we can see these principles at work. Contagious diseases introduce externalities, giving us all a stake in the health care of our neighbors and pointing toward public programs to ensure vaccination and to prevent epidemics. The generally accepted social principle that the market should not legislate matters of life and death obliges public policy to ensure at least a minimum level of medical care to all. Since the consumer faces enormous informational problems in the choice of highly complex professional medical services, the government has responsibility to set standards for practitioners and to regulate the sale of potentially harmful medicines. Since the supply of medical workers depends on the scale and mix of educational efforts, which cannot be regarded as rapidly responsive to the signals of the market, government action may be needed to shorten the time lags.

The economist has a role to play in shaping programs in such areas. Applying the tools of planning, programming, and budgeting, he can help to appraise the problems of choice in order to fulfill aims at least cost. He can work to achieve objectives with minimum impairment of individual choice. He can underline the opportunities that are sacrificed by adopting medical programs; indeed, it is surprising how often he has to point

out that, although medical care is a good thing, it does not follow that everyone ought to have unlimited amounts of it at
government expense. Surely there would be a professional consensus of economists against any public program that would
give every American as many free pairs of eyeglasses as he
would like. But there would not be widespread professional
agreement on most of the relevant issues in health policy.

In other policy areas, however, professional agreement is
greater because technical elements loom larger and ideological
considerations play a smaller role. In the case of water resources, for example, the profession has accepted criteria for
measuring costs and benefits, which, in the nature of things, are
amenable to quantification. Egalitarian considerations seem far
less significant here than in the field of health; and the scope
of the public sector is less at issue since water is clearly a public
good. In every case, the judgments of economists about policy
reflect a blend of technical analysis and social philosophy.

The Economist and Presidential Leadership

The economists in our universities and research institutions
toil in the field of values as well as that of fact and theory.
When they come to Washington, they cannot leave their ideologies behind. Indeed, they should not. Political economists
necessarily move in the realm of social values, and that is the
way they become most useful, especially as advisers to the
President. Presidential leadership consists of selecting priorities,
making commitments, identifying the aims of the nation, and
then working to fulfill them. To exercise this leadership effectively, the President needs the advice of people with diverse
professional training.

Nobody comes out of graduate school with a Ph.D. in priority
setting or applied political ideology. And yet these are major
tasks in the executive's policy making. Some group of people
is going to do this job and it should include economists. Unless
there is evidence that deep thinking about social problems can
be done best by those whose minds are uncluttered by formal

training in the social sciences, the economist should not yield this territory entirely to those with no professional background. As Gardner Ackley argued:

> ... Those in authority get plenty of advice from others who show no great delicacy in distinguishing technical questions within their competence from questions of values. The President hears from other members of his Administration, from businessmen, from labor leaders, from journalists—yes, from economists. If his economic adviser refrains from advice on the gut questions of policy, the President should and will get another one.[16]

To be effective, the adviser must operate with sensitivity and understanding of the President's values and aims. He must know the President's tastes, just as a good wife has to know how her husband takes his coffee. Thus after Kennedy pledged to "start this country moving again,"[17] his economists convinced him that a 4 percent interim target for unemployment was an appropriate translation of that goal.[18] Once that commitment was made, it had broad and pervasive implications for subsequent policy decisions. When President Johnson set forth the vision of the Great Society, his economists shaped the strategies in the war against poverty to fit. They showed how prosperity could contribute to the fulfillment of a great society. They stressed the fundamental compatibility—indeed, complementarity—of material goods and spiritual goals when some of the President's staff urged him to downplay economic considerations in order to emphasize human values. Because President Johnson wished to avoid a Robin Hood or class-struggle theme in social aid to the disadvantaged, it was important to develop programs and justifications that emphasized the long-term benefits to the entire nation from investment in

16. Gardner Ackley, "The Contribution of Economists to Policy Formation," *Journal of Finance*, Vol. 21 (May 1966), p. 176.

17. *Freedom of Communications*, Pt. 1: *The Speeches, Remarks, Press Conferences, and Statements of Senator John F. Kennedy, August 1 through November 7, 1960*, Final Report of the Senate Committee on Commerce, Prepared by its Subcommittee of the Subcommittee on Communications, S. Rept. 994, 87 Cong. 1 sess. (1961), p. 542.

18. See "The President's News Conference of March 15, 1961," in *Public Papers of the Presidents of the United States: John F. Kennedy, 1961* (1962), p. 187.

human resources. When President Nixon counseled the nation to lower its voice, his economists followed, in their pronouncements, with a stress on moderation and gradualism. President Nixon's preference for the middle of the road must influence many of the staff efforts to develop program initiatives.

Efforts to flesh out the framework of the President's leadership are of particular importance within the Executive Office of the President. Many of the top officials of other agencies in the executive branch are assigned the role of advocates within the administration. For example, the Secretary of Labor is expected to be a spokesman for manpower programs. An imaginative and energetic secretary ought to be able to generate a volume of high priority manpower programs whose costs would far exceed the amount of resources and legislative energy that can be reasonably allocated to his department. Kermit Gordon, former Director of the Bureau of the Budget, recited the warning of the bureau's very first director, General Charles G. Dawes: "Cabinet members are vice presidents in charge of spending, and as such they are the natural enemies of the President." [19] In point of fact, the members of the Cabinet serve the President by making the strongest possible case for their efforts and their programs. They also serve him by developing a special liaison with private interest groups. This pluralistic system within the administration functions very well. But it does confront the President with some hard choices, which he cannot hope to make all on his own. He needs some staff and some advisers who are not assigned a role of advocacy. Here he is bound to look to the executive office agencies, including the White House staff, the Bureau of the Budget, and the Council of Economic Advisers, to exercise a check on the pluralistic structure of the administration.

To assure this check, our presidents have selected members of the Council of Economic Advisers who were not affiliated with particular interest groups. CEA members have generally

19. Kermit Gordon, "Reflections on Spending," in John D. Montgomery and Arthur Smithies (eds.), *Public Policy,* Vol. 15 (Harvard University, Graduate School of Public Administration, 1966), p. 15 (Brookings Reprint 125).

moved into public office from a university or nonprofit research institution. To be sure, most of our leading academic economists have taken fees from private groups for consulting or speech making. Moreover, an academic or public service background is no guarantee of objectivity and impartiality, nor does private activity foreclose them. The nation has been served with distinction by economists in public service who previously practiced their profession on behalf of banks, business firms, trade associations, and labor unions. But it is added insurance when the economists sitting closest to the President have a background of concern for the public interest.[20]

The effectiveness of officials in the Executive Office depends entirely on their relationship with the President. They have no programs to run and no responsibilities or powers that they can exercise on their own. The only statutory claim that the Council of Economic Advisers has on the President's eye or ear is the writing of the Economic Report. If the President's attention to the CEA were limited to that once-a-year effort, the Council would be a most uninteresting and ineffective agency. It becomes interesting and effective to the extent that it wins his confidence.

But this confidence must flow two ways. No adviser can expect to have his advice taken all or even most of the time. If he feels in disharmony with the general position and posture of the administration, he ought to leave his job. But if he considers his job worthwhile and is to do it effectively, he must accept certain standards of loyalty. He must agree to confine battling to internal councils and cannot publicly oppose administration decisions once they are made. At most he can hope that, with the President's blessing, he may occasionally launch trial balloons and thus move in the vanguard of administration policy. Loyalty may even dictate that he prepare briefs for others to use with legitimate arguments in favor of positions with which he does not agree. He can and should maintain

20. For a contrasting view, see William H. Chartener, "The Business Economist in Government," *Business Economics,* Vol. 4 (January 1969), p. 10.

personal integrity by refusing to say publicly anything that he does not believe even though he cannot say publicly everything he does believe.

Given these constraints, members of the Council of Economic Advisers are clearly recognized as the President's men. If they speak publicly, they will be identified as spokesmen for administration positions. A Council chairman can respond to this dilemma, as Edwin Nourse and Arthur Burns did, by speaking very rarely for the public record. As Nourse strongly expressed his view:

For the President to permit or encourage intervention of Council members in any manner in the legislative process or in the public promotion of measures or policies is to make them politically expendable and to destroy the unique usefulness of the Council as an institution designed for scientific service to the executive branch.[21]

Most of the other six Council chairmen have not subscribed to this view. They have advocated and explained publicly many administration economic policies and proposals. When the President's case was their case and when the issues could be illuminated by economic education of the citizenry, they have spoken out—as partisans, but as partisans with expertise and professional integrity.

In such cases, both the speaker and the listeners know that the discussion is pursued within, and not above, the political fray. The mere fact that the Council agrees with the President can never be news and can never enhance an administration position. No CEA member has ever claimed to be the spokesman for a purely professional view. Woodrow Wilson once said with obvious facetiousness, "The trouble with the Republican party is that it has not had a new idea for thirty years. I am not speaking as a politician; I am speaking as an historian." [22] Neither presidents nor their advisers can hope ever to

21. Edwin G. Nourse, *Economics in the Public Service: Administrative Aspects of the Employment Act* (Harcourt, Brace, 1953), p. 500.

22. Albert Shaw (ed.), *President Wilson's State Papers and Addresses* (New York: Review of Reviews Co., 1917), p. 81.

convince their audiences that their pronouncements on partisan issues are professional and nonpolitical.

In short, when the President's economists decide to go on public record, they cannot serve two masters. They cannot speak both for the President and for the profession. And they cannot speak for the profession publicly and still maintain confidence and rapport internally with the President. The choice should be clear. It is far more important for society and for the profession to have economists who maintain rapport with the President and thus can have greatest influence on the inside.

A Voice for Consensus

Yet this is not an entirely satisfactory conclusion. One wishes for a more effective way of influencing public and congressional opinion in the areas of professional consensus. There is a role to be played by a Supreme Court of the profession, although a less important one than that actually fulfilled by the Council and the Bureau of the Budget in recent years.

This is not necessarily an either-or choice. One can conceive of another and separate institution outside the administration consisting of economic experts ready to speak up on policy matters involving technical results or widespread professional agreement. Somebody would have to select a group of "outside" economic experts, clearly bipartisan in composition. They could not be self-selected nor should they be named by the President. Perhaps the minority and majority leadership of the Congress could best handle this assignment; they might wish to consult with officers of the American Economic Association for suggestions. Perhaps the majority and minority might each choose six economic experts. This group of twelve could perform the specific and limited function of defining the scope of bipartisan professional agreement. They would make recommendations only when the group was nearly unanimous—perhaps ten signatures out of the twelve might be required on any report. One would expect to hear from the group only rarely on specific pieces of legislation, but it might set forth important principles and positions on both macro- and microeconomic policies. Such a group would probably have supported appropriately restrictive fiscal and monetary actions in 1966–68. It might have done considerable good, and it could hardly have done much harm.

Some risks attend the initiation of any institution in the policy process, no matter how modest its conception and objectives. If too much were expected from the advisory group in terms of either influence or specific recommendations, it could be condemned to failure. If its silence on certain issues would be viewed as incriminating, it might add further to the suspicion that economists are hopelessly divided. If this group would seem to introduce a technocratic element in policy issues or to present a picture of a medieval tribunal of wise men ruling on the theology of social issues, its creation would not serve the nation.

I am confident that it would not endanger the place of the maverick in the profession; he would still find a receptive audience. Nor would it be likely to interfere with the functions of existing institutions; indeed, it would help to clarify the fact that the Council of Economic Advisers simply cannot and should never be expected to fulfill the nonpolitical, purely professional function. In the last analysis, such a group would be beneficial only if it influenced our legislators, directly or indirectly. If they would take such a group seriously and find its judgments helpful, its creation could be a way of resolving a dilemma of the political and nonpolitical role of the economist in public policy.

Whether or not new institutions are created, there will be a continuing challenge to narrow the gap between the judgment of the profession and the law of the land. It must be demonstrated that there *is* a professional view on many matters. The day ought to come when informed noneconomists are no longer surprised that the negative income tax can be strongly advocated by "new economists" like James Tobin and Joseph Pechman and also by Milton Friedman.

To convey the professional view effectively requires the talents of a missionary, an outstanding pedagogue, and a super-salesman; it also takes skillful and sympathetic understanding of opposition views and, especially, of noneconomic considerations in policy choices. These requirements and skills differ from those most vital to successful academic research. The areas of professional consensus are rarely on the frontier of economic inquiry. They are typically built on the foundation of theoretical and empirical results that have been established and accepted by the profession long ago.

The political economist's task can be aided by some types of academic research that can nail down, dramatize, and quantify his message. But the academic researcher will rarely regard these as the most challenging scientific problems. Meanwhile, the political economist will find that much of the exploration on the frontiers of economic knowledge is irrelevant to his task of providing ammunition for the battles waged in a political arena. And so political economy has to be a separate and distinct activity of the profession. It is not science, but it is a source of potential benefit to the nation. And it will remain alive and well in Washington, whichever party occupies the White House.

chapter two

Achieving Sustained Prosperity

One of the most pleasant assignments of the Council of Economic Advisers under President Johnson was the responsibility for keeping straight the arithmetic on the duration of the nation's economic expansion. By January 1969, we were able to report that the economy had advanced for ninety-five months since the last recession ended early in 1961. Nobody asks me for that statistic any longer; but I still enjoy keeping score. As of this writing (November 1969), the nation is in its one-hundred-and-fifth month of unparalleled, unprecedented, and uninterrupted economic expansion.

Obsolescence of the Business Cycle Pattern

The persistence of prosperity has been the outstanding fact of American economic history of the 1960s. The absence of recession for nearly nine years marks a discrete and dramatic departure from the traditional performance of the American economy. Our long-term record of economic progress has been a series of two steps forward followed by one step back. Over the past century, periods of economic expansion have averaged about two and one-half years in length, ending in recession or depression. Before 1961, the longest expansion was an eighty-month period largely during the Second World War, and the holder of second place was the fifty-month extended but incomplete recovery from the Great Depression during the 1930s. The three expansions between 1948 and 1960 lasted forty-five, thirty-five, and twenty-five months.[1] Reflecting in part the built-

1. For the chronology of business cycles, see *Business Conditions Digest*.

in stabilizers of our fiscal and financial system, the postwar recessions were brief and mild as compared with the prewar record. But, until 1961, recessions were not significantly less frequent than previously. Western European nations managed to make prosperity last during the fifties, but the United States did not share this success.

According to the historical record, once the American economy pulled out of a recession, there was a safe period of approximately eighteen months during which a rebound in inventory investment virtually assured the expansion of overall activity. Once that safe period passed, it was about an even bet that an expansion would last another ten months and this estimated life expectancy applied regardless of whether the expansion had already lasted eighteen or thirty-eight months.[2]

Thus, on the basis of previous performance, the odds in February 1961 against the new expansion surviving one hundred and five months were about 400 to 1. For one hundred and eight months, the chance would have been 1/512—the compound probability of getting through nine ten-month periods after the initial safe interval, equivalent to the likelihood of a fair coin coming up heads nine times in a row.

When recessions were a regular feature of the economic environment, they were often viewed as inevitable. Indeed, the Doctor Panglosses saw them as contributors to the health of our best of all possible economies, correcting for the excesses of the boom, purging the poisons out of our productive and financial systems, and restoring vigor for new advances. And the latter-day Machiavellis saw potentially great political significance in the timing of turning points. They spun out fantasies, suggesting or suspecting—depending upon whether their party was in or out of office—that the business cycle would be controlled so that the inevitable recession would come between elections and would be replaced by a vigorous economic recovery during the campaign period.

2. Arthur M. Okun, "On the Appraisal of Cyclical Turning-Point Predictors," *Journal of Business*, Vol. 33 (April 1960), pp. 101–20.

Professional thinking about overall economic performance was also deeply rooted in the business cycle approach. It focused on our position in terms of the stage of the business cycle, attempted to diagnose how long an expansion could continue, and considered what might be done when a recession took place. Policy was often geared to the simple judgment that sustainable expansion was the good and recession was the bad in the economic tides of the nation. Economic forecasts were concentrated on finding the next turning point—the time when the economy would shift from expansion to contraction or the reverse.

The experience of the sixties has made a marked and lasting change in business cycle mentality. Since November 1968, the monthly Bureau of the Census publication of economic data carries a new title, *Business Conditions Digest,* instead of *Business Cycle Developments.* It continues to be known as BCD, but, as a sign of the times, the "Business Cycle" has disappeared. Today few research economists regard the business cycle as a particularly useful organizing framework for the overall analysis of current economic activity, and few teachers see "business cycles" as an appropriate title for a course to be offered to their students. Now virtually no one espouses the fiscal formula that was most popular with thinking conservatives just a decade ago—that of balancing the federal budget over the course of a business cycle.

In 1965 President Johnson was making a controversial statement when he said: "I do not believe recessions are inevitable." [3] That statement is no longer controversial. Recessions are now generally considered to be fundamentally preventable, like airplane crashes and unlike hurricanes. But we have not banished air crashes from the land, and it is not clear that we have the wisdom or the ability to eliminate recessions. The danger has not disappeared. The forces that produced recurrent

3. *Economic Report of the President together with the Annual Report of the Council of Economic Advisers, January 1965,* p. 10. Hereafter, this document will be referred to as *Economic Report* or *Annual Report of the CEA,* followed by the year.

recessions are still in the wings, merely waiting for their cue.

Recessions did not just happen; they reflected the vulner-ability of an industrial economy to cumulative movements up-ward and downward. While they have diverse specific causes, cyclical fluctuations can usually be viewed as the result of im-balances between the growth of productive capacity and the growth of final demands for its output. During periods of pros-perity, a significant part of the nation's output is used to in-crease productive capacity through investment in plant and equipment and in business inventories. If the growth of final demand by consumers and government keeps pace and hence sales expand, the increase in fixed and working capital normally turns out to be profitable. The expansionary decisions of busi-nessmen are thus validated, and further expansion is encour-aged. The advance then generally keeps rolling along, although it might be deterred by tight credit or unfavorable cost-price developments.

If, on the other hand, final demand fails to grow sufficiently to make use of growing capacity, businessmen have an incentive to slow down the expansion of the stocks of plant, equipment, and inventories. Even if these capital stocks continue to grow, the mere decline in the rate of expansion of capacity can mean an absolute cutback in the demand for capital goods and for output to be added to inventories. Payrolls and other incomes are thus reduced in some areas; in turn, these income declines lead to more widespread reductions in spending and may gener-ate a decline in total demand. Thus a slowdown in economic activity may be converted into an absolute downturn—a reces-sion or depression.

The balance between final buying and stock building can be upset on either side. Overbuilding of inventories apparently played a key role in the first postwar downturn in 1948. A sharp decline in the government's final demand for defense products precipitated the second postwar recession in 1953. In 1956–57, final demand grew very slowly while productive capacity was expanding rapidly in a major boom for capital goods. In 1959–60, when fiscal and monetary policies were very restrictive, final demand grew too slowly to support even the moderate expansion of capacity that was taking place. Various imbalances have also developed at times in the 1960s, but they have never become so large or so widespread as to turn the economy down. The nature of economic fluctuations has not changed; policies to contain them have made the difference.

The record of economic advance in the sixties has been impressive in strength as well as length. As we caught up and kept up with our productive capacity in eight and one-half years of expansion, our real output grew 51 percent, or 5.0 percent a year, in contrast with our long-term annual average of 3 percent. Real disposable income per capita—our best price-corrected measure of the purchasing power of the average consumer—rose one-third, as much of a gain as in the preceding nineteen years. Corporate profits doubled. The number of civilian jobs increased more than 12 million, enough to match the growth of the labor force and to reduce unemployment by more than 2 million persons.[4]

The record presents a striking contrast to the sluggish growth and recurrent recessions of the late fifties. From 1953 to 1960, the growth of industrial production in the United States averaged only 2.5 percent a year, below the pace of every other industrial nation. Between 1956 and 1961, real gross national product (GNP) rose at an average rate of 2.1 percent, so far below the 6.4 percent estimated rate of the Soviet Union [5] that it made credible Khrushchev's threat to "bury" us economically. In June 1962, Gunnar Myrdal identified as "the world's greatest problem" neither peace nor race relations, but "economic stagnation" in America.[6]

As the economy entered the sixties staggering rather than soaring, observers drew cosmic implications from its unsatisfactory performance. Some saw it as hopelessly stagnant, arguing

4. Figures on aggregate economic activity are official government statistics, generally produced by either the Department of Commerce or the Department of Labor, and will not be individually footnoted.

5. *Soviet Economic Performance: 1966–67,* Materials Prepared for the Subcommittee on Foreign Economic Policy of the Joint Economic Committee, 90 Cong. 2 sess. (1968), p. 12.

6. *Washington Post,* June 9, 1962.

that automation and technical progress had altered labor requirements so much as to make high employment an impossibility. We heard dire forecasts raising the specter of automation, the threat of the "triple revolution," [7] the prospect of persistent structural deterioration of labor markets. Thus Robert Theobald predicted:

> Unemployment rates must therefore be expected to rise in the sixties. This unemployment will be concentrated among the unskilled, the older worker and the youngster entering the labor force. Minority groups will also be hard hit. No conceivable rate of economic growth will avoid this result. [8]

In fact, of course, unemployment has fallen sharply during the 1960s. As shown in Figure 1, unemployment rates in the spring of 1969 were not only dramatically lower than in the first quarter of 1961 but also well below those of the spring of 1959, one of the most prosperous quarters of the late fifties. Although teenagers remained victims of high unemployment rates, particularly impressive gains were made by adults who had been at the back of the hiring line.

The attitudes of the early sixties seem dim today. This is proof *par excellence* that at least some controversies in economics get resolved. It also reveals the dangers of cosmic generalizations based on a limited period of experience. Predictions of a chronic dollar shortage, chronic stagnation, chronic secular deterioration in labor markets, and the like have all been sounded in the past generation. And all have been refuted by subsequent developments. Yet the lessons seem to go unheeded. We now see the start of a new wave of cosmic generalizations centering on perpetual inflation, perpetual strength of investment demand, and perpetual credit scarcity. This new wave may already have influenced policy by serving as an intellectual justification for the permanent repeal of the investment tax credit. It will be surprising if the new generalizations hold up much better than their predecessors.

7. *New York Times,* March 23, 1964. The triple revolution entails cybernation, weaponry, and human rights.

8. Robert Theobald, "Abundance: Threat or Promise?" *The Nation,* May 11, 1963, p. 394.

The New Strategy of Economic Policy

More vigorous and more consistent application of the tools of economic policy contributed to the obsolescence of the business cycle pattern and the refutation of the stagnation myths. The reformed strategy of economic policy did not rest on any new theory: Ever since Keynes, economists had recognized that the federal government could stimulate economic activity by increasing the injection of federal expenditures into the income stream or by reducing the withdrawal of federal tax receipts. For generations they had noted the influence of the cost and availability of credit on expenditures financed with borrowed funds.

Nor were the tools of policy new and different. Some stimulative fiscal actions had been taken under the aegis of the New Deal in the 1930s. The Employment Act of 1946 declared the federal government's continuing responsibility to promote "maximum employment, production, and purchasing power," [9] relying mainly on fiscal and monetary devices. During each of the four postwar recessions, some countercyclical fiscal and monetary measures had been adopted; and each period of inflationary boom had been met with some counteracting policies of economic restraint.[10]

Until the 1960s, however, the use of the federal budget for purposes of economic stabilization often followed a fire-fighting strategy. Deliberate stimulus or restraint through budget deficits or substantial surpluses was applied only when the alarm sounded. At other times, the orthodox rule of balancing the budget seemed to dominate. And because the deliberate application of fiscal policy was widely viewed as an emergency measure, there were considerable inhibitions about initiating a policy program. Any time the President proposed budgetary measures designed to serve economic objectives, he was con-

9. 60 Stat. 23.
10. For a detailed, scholarly treatment of the history of fiscal policy, see Herbert Stein, *The Fiscal Revolution in America* (University of Chicago Press, 1969).

Figure 1. *Unemployment Rates for Selected Groups, Spring 1959, Winter 1961, and Spring 1969* [a]

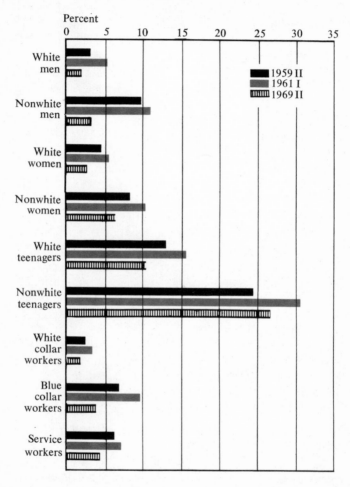

Source: U.S. Department of Labor.

a. Data for men and women are for persons 20 years old and over; data for teenagers for persons 16 to 19 years old.

ceding that the economy was in an emergency and needed the fire department for a rescue operation. That inhibition contributed to delays in the adoption of appropriate antirecessionary measures in each of the four postwar slumps. Similarly, there was eagerness to return to business-as-usual once the recession emergency ended.

These attitudes were particularly pronounced in the late 1950s. Thus, with the unemployment rate near 6 percent, President Eisenhower said in his State of the Union Message of January 1959, "If we cannot live within our means during such a time of rising prosperity, the hope for fiscal integrity will fade." [11] In recalling a decision of the Eisenhower administration not to reverse its restrictive fiscal program early in 1960, Richard Nixon reported, ". . . There was strong sentiment against using the spending and credit powers of the Federal Government to affect the economy, unless and until conditions clearly indicated a major recession in prospect." [12] As Mr. Nixon's summary makes clear, the restrictive fiscal policy of 1959–60 should not be construed as a conscious and deliberate effort to stop growth in order to eliminate inflationary expectations.[13] Surely, the 1960–61 recession was not intentionally planned by the Eisenhower administration. Nor was a 5 percent rate of unemployment regarded as a minimum for the nation. To be sure, risks were consciously taken on the side of excessive restraint, but these corresponded to the preference for orthodox budgetary principles that largely ignored the economic impact of fiscal policy. The basic strategy was to stick with orthodox principles unless the fire alarm of recession tolled

11. *Public Papers of the Presidents of the United States: Dwight D. Eisenhower, 1959* (1960), p. 12.

12. Richard M. Nixon, *Six Crises* (Doubleday, 1962), p. 310.

13. In *Fiscal Revolution,* Herbert Stein notes this hypothesis, quoting Samuelson's reference to the "investment in sadism by the second Eisenhower Administration" (p. 506). But Samuelson made clear his judgment that the "investment" stemmed from "inactivism and errors of omission" rather than a deliberate choice to abort economic growth. Arthur F. Burns and Paul A. Samuelson, *Full Employment, Guideposts and Economic Stability* (Washington: American Enterprise Institute for Public Policy Research, 1967), p. 87.

loud and clear. This ruled out the use of stimulative—or even supportive—fiscal policies during periods of expansion.

In the late forties and early fifties, the possible need for stimulative policies even during expansionary periods was widely discussed.[14] But events did not put this strategy to the test during the first postwar decade. Spurred by the Korean buildup in 1950, the economy rose swiftly to—and beyond—full employment in its recovery from the first postwar recession. Again in 1954–55, the rebound from recession was strong and prompt, carrying the nation to essentially full utilization by the close of 1955. From that point on, however, expansion and full utilization did not go hand in hand. The growth of output was very sluggish during the last year and a half of the 1954–57 expansion. Even at its peak in the spring of 1960, the recovery from the 1957–58 recession left the economy far short of full employment. These experiences highlighted the distinction between high employment and cyclical expansion.

Against this background, the strategy of economic policy was reformulated in the sixties. The revised strategy emphasized, as the standard for judging economic performance, whether the economy was living up to its potential rather than merely whether it was advancing. Ideally, total demand should be in balance with the nation's supply capabilities. When the balance is achieved, there is neither the waste of idle resources nor the strain of inflationary pressure. The nation is then actually producing its potential output. The concept of potential output was imprecise and so was its quantification. Yet it helped to deliver and dramatize the verdict that idle resources were a major national extravagance in the late fifties and early sixties. And the

14. See, for example, *Economic Report, 1953*, esp. pp. 14–24; Gerhard Colm, "The Federal Budget and the National Economy," in National Planning Association, *The Need for Further Budget Reform*, Planning Pamphlets, 90 (Washington: NPA, 1955), esp. pp. 55–59; Leon H. Keyserling, "The Council of Economic Advisers' Tasks in the Next Decade," in Gerhard Colm (ed.), *The Employment Act, Past and Future—A Tenth Anniversary Symposium*, Special Report 41 (Washington: National Planning Association, 1956), pp. 67–73.

quantification, which had been heatedly debated in 1961,[15] held up surprisingly well during the sixties, as Figure 2 indicates.

The shift of emphasis from the achievement of expansion to the realization of potential had a number of important corollaries. First, by establishing a moving target for economic performance, it stressed the growth of the economy. The supply capabilities of the United States economy advance continually, reflecting both our expanding labor force and the improving productivity that results from advancing technology and investment in human and physical resources. In the late fifties, the growth of potential had amounted to about 3½ percent per year; the shortfall of actual performance below that pace showed up in rising unemployment. The actual growth performance was unsatisfactory because it failed to take full advantage of our growing supply capabilities, even though new record highs in income and employment were achieved.

Second, the focus on the gap between potential and actual output provided a new scale for the evaluation of economic performance, replacing the dichotomized business cycle standard which viewed expansion as satisfactory and recession as unsatisfactory. This new scale of evaluation, in turn, led to greater activism in economic policy: As long as the economy was not realizing its potential, improvement was needed and government had a responsibility to promote it.

Finally, the promotion of expansion along the path of poten-

15. See, for example, the statement of the Council of Economic Advisers, "The American Economy in 1961: Problems and Policies," and testimony of Walter W. Heller, Chairman, in *January 1961 Economic Report of the President and the Economic Situation and Outlook,* Hearings before the Joint Economic Committee, 87 Cong. 1 sess. (1961), pp. 290–419; Arthur M. Okun, "Potential GNP: Its Measurement and Significance," in American Statistical Association, *Proceedings of the Business and Economic Statistics Section* (1962), pp. 98–104, reprinted in the Appendix; and exchange of Arthur Burns with the Council of Economic Advisers: Arthur F. Burns, "Examining the New 'Stagnation' Theory," reply by the Council of Economic Advisers, "The Council's View," and rebuttal by Burns, "A Second Look at the Council's Economic Theory," published in *Morgan Guaranty Survey,* May 1961, pp. 1–7, and August 1961, pp. 1–6 and 6–15, respectively.

Figure 2. *Gross National Product, Actual and Potential, and Unemployment Rates, 1955–68*

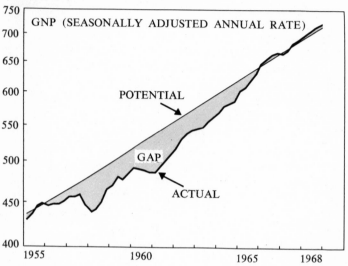

Billions of 1958 dollars
(ratio scale)

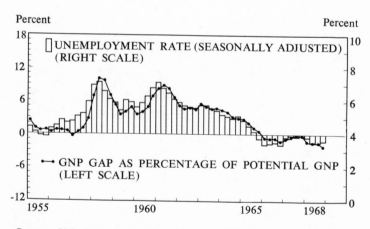

Source: U.S. Department of Commerce, U.S. Department of Labor, and Council of Economic Advisers.

tial was viewed as the best defense against recession. Two recessions emerged in the 1957–60 period because expansions had not had enough vigor to be self-sustaining. The slow advance failed to make full use of existing capital; hence, incentives to invest deteriorated and the economy turned down. In light of the conclusion that anemic recoveries are likely to die young, the emphasis was shifted from curative to preventive measures. The objective was to promote brisk advance in order to make prosperity durable and self-sustaining.

All of this added up to a coherent view of stabilization policy. Something here was new and different. Arthur Burns has summarized it perceptively:

> The central doctrine of this school is that the stage of the business cycle has little relevance to sound economic policy; that policy should be growth-oriented instead of cycle-oriented; that the vital matter is whether a gap exists between actual and potential output; that fiscal deficits and monetary tools need to be used to promote expansion when a gap exists; and that the stimuli should be sufficient to close the gap—provided significant inflationary pressures are not whipped up in the process.[16]

The adoption of these principles led to a more active stabilization policy. The activist strategy was the key that unlocked the door to sustained expansion in the 1960s. The record of economic performance shows serious blemishes, particularly the inflation since 1966. To some degree, these reflect errors of analysis and prediction by economists; to a larger degree, however, they reflect errors of omission in failing to implement the activist strategy.

The expansion can be divided into two distinct parts, which are discussed in some detail below. The remainder of this chapter is devoted to the period from early 1961 until mid-1965, when the main task was to invigorate the economy. The major problem could be simply and clearly diagnosed as inadequate total demand, and the equally simple remedy was stimulative fiscal and monetary policy. By mid-1965, that diagnosis had

16. Burns, in a dialogue with Samuelson, *Full Employment, Guideposts and Economic Stability,* pp. 31–32.

become accepted and much of the remedy had been applied.

Thereafter, the assignment was to hold to a course of noninflationary prosperity, a problem for which the economist does not have a simple and satisfactory solution. It is inherently a much more difficult task, and it was made ever so much more difficult by large increases in defense spending. The record after mid-1965 is reviewed in Chapter 3.

Onward and Upward

As Walter Heller has said: "In 1961, with over five million unemployed and a production gap of nearly $50 billion, the problem of the economic adviser was not what to say, but how to get people to listen." [17] The appropriate remedy required— at least for a time—budgetary deficits and increases in the national debt. There was widespread professional agreement on this prescription. In Herbert Stein's judgment, "If [President Kennedy] had chosen six American economists at random the odds were high that he would have obtained five with the ideas on fiscal policy which his advisers actually had, because those ideas were shared by almost all economists in 1960." [18]

Outside the profession, however, antipathy toward such unorthodox federal budgeting was deeply entrenched; it had been strongly nurtured during the fifties, and remained an obstacle to rational action in 1961. John F. Kennedy had not challenged the orthodox principles during the 1960 election campaign; indeed, he had criticized President Eisenhower's $12 billion budgetary deficit of fiscal 1959. [19] President Kennedy bent but did not break the traditional rules in taking steps to invigorate

17. Walter W. Heller, *New Dimensions of Political Economy* (Harvard University Press, 1966; W. W. Norton, 1967), p. 27.

18. Stein, *Fiscal Revolution*, p. 380.

19. See, for example, *Freedom of Communications*, Pt. 1: *The Speeches, Remarks, Press Conferences, and Statements of Senator John F. Kennedy, August 1 through November 7, 1960,* Final Report of the Senate Committee on Commerce, Prepared by its Subcommittee of the Subcommittee on Communications, S. Rept. 994, 87 Cong. 1 sess. (1961), p. 1077.

recovery during 1961 and in heeding the advice of his economists that the Berlin defense buildup did not call for higher taxes. Then the President bowed to the orthodox rules in January 1962, proposing a balanced budget at a time when 6 percent of the labor force was unemployed.[20]

It was only when the expansion faltered in the spring of 1962 that Kennedy reached a fork in the fiscal road. In a memorable commencement address at Yale University in June 1962, he spoke out clearly and strongly against budgetary orthodoxy:

> The myth persists that Federal deficits create inflation and budget surpluses prevent it. . . . Obviously deficits are sometimes dangerous —and so are surpluses. But honest assessment plainly required a more sophisticated view than the old and automatic cliché that deficits automatically bring inflation. . . .
> . . . What we need is not labels and clichés but more basic discussion of the sophisticated and technical questions involved in keeping a great economic machine moving ahead.[21]

Once President Kennedy called this play, Walter Heller carried the ball and brought the "sophisticated and technical questions" before the public. The press served as the textbook for the biggest course in elementary macroeconomics ever presented. In fact, Professor Heller captured his millions of students with new labels in place of old. The "full employment surplus," "constructive deficit," "fiscal dividend and fiscal drag," and "output gap" were drummed home in repeated lessons. The message was effectively conveyed to the business and financial community and to the nation's legislators by the Secretary of the Treasury, C. Douglas Dillon, and then Under Secretary Henry H. Fowler.

The administrative reform of depreciation guidelines and the enactment of the investment tax credit in 1962 were two new policy initiatives which directly stimulated business investment and made their largest direct contribution to business incomes.

20. For an interesting account of this period, see James L. Sundquist, *Politics and Policy: The Eisenhower, Kennedy, and Johnson Years* (Brookings Institution, 1968), pp. 34–46.
21. *Public Papers of the Presidents of the United States: John F. Kennedy, 1962* (1963), pp. 472–73.

It was probably no coincidence that the first installment of the expansionary strategy worked to benefit directly the groups that seemed particularly hostile to a heterodox, deficit-prone fiscal policy. Remarkably, the proposed investment tax credit was initially viewed as a Grecian gift by many businessmen; their support was enlisted through a major educational effort led by Under Secretary Fowler.

The next stage was bigger, bolder, and more progressive in its distributive impact. Facing up to legislative realities, President Kennedy decided not to ask for an immediate general tax reduction in the summer of 1962. But in August he publicly announced that he would propose a substantial tax reduction in January 1963.

The tax-cut proposal was designed by economists and promoted by economists on economic grounds. As Heller has explained, the size of the proposed tax reduction was based on careful and quantitative professional judgment—although hardly a scientific determination—of that amount of fiscal stimulus appropriate to close the remaining gap between the potential and actual output.[22] With the envisioned shift in fiscal policy, the federal budget would come into approximate balance when the nation attained its potential output, but it would no longer dampen demand with large surpluses at full employment. In addition to the rate reductions, the tax package included many proposals for significant reform of the tax structure to improve equity and efficiency. These reform proposals undoubtedly contributed to the long delay in the enactment of the tax reduction; but, more generally, there was no political consensus during 1963 in favor of the new strategy of relaxing fiscal restraint. While tax reduction was rarely opposed in principle, support for it was sometimes linked to sharp cutbacks in federal outlays that would have vitiated the intent to provide significant fiscal stimulus.

When the tax cut was finally enacted under President Johnson's leadership in February 1964, it was unprecedented in many respects. It was the largest stimulative fiscal action ever

22. Heller, *New Dimensions,* p. 72.

undertaken by the federal government in peacetime, cutting individual income tax liabilities by almost one-fifth and corporate tax bills by one-tenth. In combination with the two 1962 tax actions, the new measure reduced the effective rate of corporate taxes by one-fifth compared with its 1961 level. The 1964 tax cut was progressive in its distributive effects. In part, this was the result of the only two significant reforms that were enacted —the minimum standard deduction and the repeal of the dividend credit. In part, it resulted from the slash in the lowest tax rate from 20 to 14 percent, associated with the splitting of the bottom bracket into four segments.[23]

The big tax cut was the first major stimulative measure adopted in the postwar era at a time when the economy was neither in, nor threatened imminently by, recession. And, unlike U.S. tax reductions in the 1920s, late 1940s, and 1954, the 1964 action was taken in a budgetary situation marked by the twin facts that the federal budget was in deficit and federal expenditures were rising.

The tax cut added to demand by leaving more purchasing power in the hands of consumers and businesses. Consumers responded by spending most of that extra income for added goods and services. For businessmen investment became both more profitable and easier to finance out of internal funds. The direct stimulus of the tax cut was multiplied over time. The extra spending it generated meant more jobs and hence more incomes for many families; it strengthened markets and thus encouraged greater investment to expand capacity.

The stimulus of tax reduction dominated the economic scene in 1964 and the first half of 1965. The unemployment rate, which had been fluctuating aimlessly in the range between 5½ and 6 percent all during 1962 and 1963, fell to 5 percent during the course of 1964 and declined further to 4.7 percent during the spring of 1965. The time series on consumer spending registered a sharp take-off early in 1964. According to my

23. Joseph A. Pechman, "Individual Income Tax Provisions of the Revenue Act of 1964," *Journal of Finance,* Vol. 20 (May 1965), pp. 247–72 (Brookings Reprint 96).

estimates, the tax cut added $24 billion (annual rate) to our GNP by the second quarter of 1965, and ultimately provided a lift of $36 billion.[24]

The Revenue Act of 1964 provided for two stages of tax reduction: The first was effective in 1964 and the second took place at the beginning of 1965. Beyond the second-stage tax cut, the January 1965 budget program shifted into neutral gear. A major phased reduction of excise taxes was slated to begin at mid-year, and a stimulative liberalization of social security benefits was also envisioned. But other federal budgetary expenditures were expected to grow very little, and defense spending was scheduled to continue downward. Indeed, according to the budget plan, fiscal policy was to shift moderately toward restraint in the first half of 1966 when social security taxes were to rise. There was no new net injection of economic stimulus, and no further downward trend in the budgetary surplus as measured at full employment. As stated by the Council in January 1965: ". . . The rate of economic advance in the next eighteen months will reflect, to an increasing degree, the strength of private demand. The record of this period should test the economy's ability to advance in high gear with a small, but no longer declining, full-employment surplus." [25]

The economy seemed to be passing the initial stage of that test with flying colors in the first half of 1965. Private demand was somewhat more vigorous than had been anticipated, although not so strong as to cause serious concern. Both consumer spending and business investment forged ahead, and unemployment moved down. Revenue gains from higher personal and corporate incomes flowed into the Treasury, and brought the federal budget into surplus (on a national accounts basis) during the first half of the year. Meanwhile, in May 1965, the duration of economic expansion toppled the previous peacetime record of fifty months.

24. Arthur M. Okun, "Measuring the Impact of the 1964 Tax Reduction," in Walter W. Heller (ed.), *Perspectives on Economic Growth* (Random House, 1968).

25. *Annual Report of the CEA, 1965,* p. 100.

The nation's balance-of-payments deficit remained a nagging problem, and the quality of some types of credit gave cause for uneasiness. There was also concern lest complacency develop about the economy; this was expressed by the Chairman of the Federal Reserve when he reminded us of "disquieting similarities" between the existing economic scene and that of the late 1920s.[26] Nonetheless, any danger of complacency reflected the exceedingly desirable state of economic activity. After tolerating a high cost of wasted resources and lost output during 1962–63, the nation had finally unleashed the private economy.

The price-cost record of the economy was also generally reassuring, although it was flashing some caution signs by mid-1965. The average of wholesale industrial prices was within 1 percent of its level at the beginning of 1961. It had risen 0.5 percent during the course of 1964, mostly because of nonferrous metals prices, which were pushed up by world supply problems. During the first half of 1965, industrial wholesale prices rose 0.6 percent, with increases more widely dispersed. In manufacturing industries with rapidly rising productivity, price declines, which had previously been common, were going out of style. Yet very few large firms with market power were raising prices to widen profit margins; and there had been no further confrontation between business and government like that in April 1962 when President Kennedy had strongly condemned an increase in steel prices.

Labor costs were remarkably stable in both organized and unorganized areas. In the spring of 1965, unit labor costs in both the total nonfinancial corporate sector of the economy and in manufacturing were *below* their levels of a year earlier. Productivity advanced briskly and wage rates rose only modestly; thus unit labor costs behaved very well, even though the amount of work paid for at premium overtime rates had expanded significantly. Consumer prices were rising moderately by about

26. William McChesney Martin, Jr., "Monetary History and International Policy," *Columbia University Forum*, Vol. 8 (Summer 1965), pp. 4–9.

1½ percent per year—only a trifle more than in 1960–63—and the price deflator for overall gross national product was advancing at a 1¾ percent rate.

To be sure, the price record of 1964 and the first half of 1965 was distinctly different from that of earlier years. But it had been recognized all along that the achievement of a high-employment economy would necessarily involve some retreat from the exceptional price stability of the early sixties. When the slack in resource utilization was taken up, it was no surprise to find a departure from the virtually absolute stability of industrial wholesale prices that had ruled in earlier years. The deterioration in our price performance seemed relatively small and readily tolerable. This was not inflation by any definition I know.[27]

The 1964–65 price record generally confirmed the judgment that the Council had made way back in 1961 that an unemployment rate of 4 percent was an appropriate interim target for full utilization of manpower, consistent with the maintenance of a reasonable degree of price stability. It was felt that the achievement of a 4 percent unemployment rate along a smooth path of advance might be accompanied by a 2 percent rate of overall price increase. Such a rate would not be dramatically more rapid than the 1960–63 performance; it seemed likely to be acceptable to the nation and would not be so large as to feed on itself and accelerate through time. Thus in the spring of 1965, the President's Troika—the fiscal advisory group consisting of officials of the Treasury, the Budget Bureau, and the Council of Economic Advisers—was looking ahead to fiscal year 1967 and shaping a program to promote a

27. For a contrasting view on this issue, see Arthur F. Burns, "The Perils of Inflation," in Arthur F. Burns, *The Business Cycle in a Changing World* (Columbia University Press for the National Bureau of Economic Research, 1969). Burns concluded, "Clearly, inflation had already taken hold and become widespread many months before Vietnam began adding appreciably to aggregate monetary demand" (pp. 287–88). Burns stresses the 3 percent rise in overall wholesale prices between June 1964 and June 1965. A temporary jump in farm prices was the main element in that result, however.

continuing advance in real output that would bring the unemployment rate gradually down to the 4 percent target.

The prospects for achieving noninflationary high employment had to be viewed in many dimensions. Excise tax cuts were a particularly appropriate form of fiscal stimulus since they countered upward cost pressures. The advance in plant and equipment outlays seemed likely to strengthen our productivity performance. Several newly launched manpower programs were expected to help avoid bottlenecks in labor markets. Moreover, as labor markets began to firm, private business management intensified its own efforts to upgrade and train manpower in ways that would effectively increase both the quality and quantity of our labor supply over the long run. The vigor of foreign competition was another encouraging anti-inflationary sign.

Finally, as one element of the total program, public education on the need for price and wage restraint in areas of market power—the administration's guidepost policy—seemed to be having a favorable influence on decisions by big business and big labor.

The guideposts, first formulated by the Council of Economic Advisers in 1962, were meant to help avoid repetition of the experience in 1956–57 when price-cost stability deteriorated badly in areas of market power. They stressed the arithmetic truth that price stability could be maintained only insofar as gains in money income per unit of input remained within the bounds of advances in national productivity. This formula pointed toward increases of a little more than 3 percent a year in wage rates, paralleling the trend growth of productivity, and toward pricing policies that were geared to unit costs. The guideposts were intended to influence the decisions of large corporations and large unions by enlisting the force of public opinion against the discretionary use of market power to promote inflation. It is impossible to tell just how much influence they had in 1962–65, but there is considerable evidence that they deserve some credit.[28]

28. See John Sheahan, *The Wage-Price Guideposts* (Brookings Institution, 1967), esp. pp. 79–95; George L. Perry, "Wages and the Guide-

The Recipe for Fiscal Stimulus

The heavy reliance on tax cuts, rather than expenditure increases, in providing fiscal stimulus was a particularly interesting feature of the period. For the first time in history, an expansionary fiscal strategy was pursued without enlarging the relative size of federal expenditures in our economy. From the fourth quarter of 1960 to the second quarter of 1965, the federal sector was the slowest growing major area of the economy. While our gross national product rose 34 percent, total federal outlays—purchases, transfer payments, and so forth—increased 26 percent, or $25 billion. Federal purchases of goods and services were up 20 percent. National defense purchases rose only 7 percent.

Changes in tax laws contributed a net total of $12 billion to the annual rate of private purchasing power by the spring of 1965. Even after increases in social security taxes are netted out, tax cuts provided a third of the total gross stimulative actions undertaken during the four-and-one-half-year period. They accounted for two-thirds of the gross stimulus during the initial one and one-half years of the Johnson presidency, as total federal outlays rose only $5 billion from the last quarter of 1963 to the second quarter of 1965.

This heavy reliance on tax reduction reflected neither an economic judgment on the relative efficacy of the two types of fiscal stimuli nor the administration's assessment of national priorities, but rather the political constraints of the day. A deficit budget might be tolerated by the nation if it stressed tax reduc-

posts," *American Economic Review,* Vol. 57 (September 1967), pp. 897–904, comments by Paul S. Anderson, Michael L. Wachter, and Adrian W. Throop, and reply by Perry, *American Economic Review,* Vol. 59 (June 1969), pp. 351–70; Otto Eckstein, "Money Wage Determination Revisited," *Review of Economic Studies,* Vol. 35 (April 1968), pp. 133–43; and Robert M. Solow, "The Wage-Price Issue and the Guideposts," in Frederick H. Harbison and Joseph D. Mooney (eds.), *Critical Issues in Employment Policy,* A Report of the Princeton Manpower Symposium, May 12–13, 1966 (Princeton University, 1966), pp. 57–73.

tion; it would be much less popular if it featured rapid increases in government spending. Moreover, a crusade for enlarged social programs seemed to have no prospect of success. Indeed, it could not have been launched by simply requesting additional appropriations for existing programs; most of the key authorizing legislation underlying current major social efforts in education, housing, manpower, and health was not yet on the statute books in 1963. The makers of fiscal policy believed that additional federal outlays could add equally well to total demand, but they did not regard this as a realistic alternative. The real choice was between tax cuts and no fiscal stimulus at all.

The Fiscal-Monetary Partnership

The stimulus to the economy also reflected a unique partnership between fiscal and monetary policy. Basically, monetary policy was accommodative while fiscal policy was the active partner. The Federal Reserve allowed the demands for liquidity and credit generated by a rapidly expanding economy to be met at stable interest rates. The stability was neither perfect nor complete because of the concern that very low short-term interest rates would worsen our balance-of-payments performance. Hence short rates, such as those on Treasury bills, were nudged upward whenever additional capital outflows seemed to be encouraged by a widening gap between domestic and foreign yields in money markets. Remarkably, this proved to be possible without a major upward impact on the longer-term interest rates that seem to be most important to domestic spending. As Figure 3 indicates, long-term yields were far more stable in the early sixties than in the late fifties. While the Federal Reserve obviously did not "peg" bond yields, it did aim to stabilize longer-term interest rates. The resulting increases in the quantity of money, bank credit, business loans, and total borrowing all reflected shifts in demands for funds with an essentially passive response on the supply side.

This rate-oriented posture was a major departure from tradition. In previous periods of significant economic expansion, the

Figure 3. *Selected Interest Rates, 1957–65*

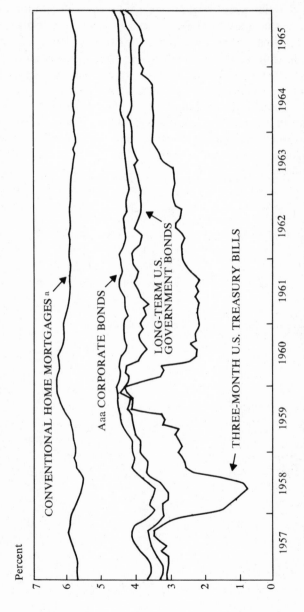

Sources: Federal Reserve Board, U.S. Treasury Department, Federal Housing Administration.
a. Before April 1960, new and existing homes; after that date, new homes only.

Federal Reserve had not allowed the supply of credit to expand in pace with growing demands, and interest rates had tended to rise. Monetary policy had thus acted to moderate and contain expansions. But the Fed did not "lean against the wind" during 1961–65. As long as the economy continued to operate below its potential and prices remained stable, the Fed was prepared to provide the liquidity to sustain the advance.

Milton Friedman has attributed to monetary policy the chief causal role in stimulating the expansion of that period. Indeed, he argues:

> . . . So far as I know, there has been no empirical demonstration that that tax cut [the 1964 reduction] had any effect on the total flow of income in the U.S. There has been no demonstration that if monetary policies had been maintained unchanged . . . the tax cut would have been really expansionary on nominal income. . . .
>
> What Okun did [in an analysis of the tax cut] was to assume away the whole problem because he looked only at the effect of fiscal policy without asking what role monetary policy played during that period.[29]

Friedman's critique raises, first of all, a conceptual issue of whether my study of the impact of the tax cut did "assume away the whole problem." In trying to provide a meaningful answer to the common sense question of what impact the tax cut had on economic activity, one has to make some assumptions about what monetary policy would have been if the tax cut had not been enacted. Monetary conditions are merely one of the many assumptions that must be specified in assessing the impact of the tax bill. It is also necessary, for example, to assume what would have happened to federal expenditures if the tax reduction had not taken place. In my paper, I assumed that they would have been exactly what they were in fact. This, of course, is an arbitrary assumption, but it is a reasonable way to focus on the impact of the tax cut.

The assumptions about monetary factors seem equally rea-

29. Milton Friedman and Walter W. Heller, *Monetary vs. Fiscal Policy* (W. W. Norton, 1969), p. 55. Friedman refers to my paper, "Measuring the Impact of the 1964 Tax Reduction."

sonable. It is factually clear that the Federal Reserve had conducted an accommodative monetary policy before the tax cut,
and that it continued to pursue an accommodative monetary
policy for a year and a half afterwards. Both preceding and
following the enactment of the tax cut, monetary strategy was
geared to provide the reserves needed to stabilize interest rates
and the availability of credit. In that sense, monetary policy was
unchanged by the tax cut, and I assumed it would have been
unchanged if there had been no tax cut. Since interest rates remained remarkably stable during the entire period, it seems
reasonable to assume that, in the absence of the tax cut, they
would also have been kept stable by an accommodative, rate-
oriented monetary policy.

Of course, because of the tax cut, the unchanged rate-oriented
monetary policy accommodated a more rapid growth of demand for funds and, hence, provided more growth of the money
supply, bank credit, and other related financial flows than
would have taken place without the tax cut. An interesting and
perfectly reasonable statistical exercise could explore what
would have happened after the tax cut if the Federal Reserve
had shifted strategy and decided not to accommodate the extra
demands for funds. But that exercise is not the way to assess
the impact of the tax cut of 1964.

Perhaps this analogy will help. During the early sixties, the
Federal Reserve took the position of a ticket seller ready to sell
tickets at a fixed price to anyone on line. Given this policy, sales
of tickets were determined by the number of people who got on
line. One cannot explain adequately why more people saw a
show by saying that the ticket seller sold more tickets (at a
given price). It doesn't make any more sense to say that the
economic stimulus in 1964–65 came from a change in monetary policy. The tax cut does explain why more people got in
line; given the willingness of the ticket seller to expand his sales,
activity increased. I was concerned with estimating the magnitude of that expansion and, hence, had no reason to ask what
would have happened if the ticket seller had refused to sell more
tickets.

All of this relates entirely to the issue of whether my study of the tax cut asked the right question, not whether it gave the proper answer to the question it asked. In any comparison of two situations, both involving an accommodative, rate-oriented monetary policy but one with a tax cut and one without it, Friedman would not disagree, to the best of my knowledge, that the tax cut situation would be associated with a higher gross national product.[30]

There are a number of other empirical judgments in comparing hypothetical situations on which "new economists" and "monetarists" can agree. For one thing, I believe that the success of the fiscal strategy depended on the monetary response. If, when the tax cut was enacted, our ticket seller had been reluctant to issue more tickets, interest rates would have risen rather than remaining stable, and credit availability would have been restricted; GNP would then have moved along a lower path than the one that actually resulted. Surely the Fed could have imposed a sufficiently restrictive monetary policy to nullify entirely the expansionary effects of the tax cut.

Moreover, I have no reason to doubt that, in principle, there existed a monetary route to high employment as an alternative to the fiscal route that was traveled. As much additional demand as resulted from the tax cut could have been generated, without fiscal support, by a sufficiently aggressive Federal Reserve policy to increase liquidity and reduce interest rates.

30. For the professional technicians in the house, these points can be most readily discussed in terms of the Hicksian apparatus of the IS and LM curves. An accommodative or rate-oriented monetary policy fixes the interest rate and makes the LM curve horizontal in the relevant range. There is no dispute among economists that a permanent tax cut (or an increase in most types of government expenditures) shifts the IS curve. Given a horizontal LM curve, a shift in the IS curve necessarily changes the level of income. The elasticity of the marginal efficiency of capital and the elasticity of the demand for money with respect to the rate of interest determine the changes in the money supply associated with shifts in the IS curve; these elasticities cannot affect income or interest when the LM curve is horizontal. Whether the Fed *should* pursue a rate-oriented policy that produces a horizontal LM curve is not the issue. The fact is that it *did* in 1963, 1964, and the first half of 1965.

The monetary route would have involved significantly lower interest rates. As a political judgment, I am confident that the route would not have been traveled, given the constraints of the balance of payments on lowering interest rates as they were viewed—rightly or wrongly—by the administration and the Federal Reserve. But that is a political judgment.

One can get a debate on empirical economic issues between a monetarist and a new economist by asking whether the monetary route to full employment without the tax cut would have involved the *same* growth of the money supply that in fact took place along the fiscal route. While both would agree that the no-tax-cut situation would have involved lower interest rates, the monetarist would deny that it would have required a larger money supply than was actually experienced. According to the monetarist, we got the GNP we did because of the size of the money supply; and *that* level of total spending for output would have come from *that* money supply regardless of interest rates.

I do not regard this as a very exciting question, but I do have great confidence that the monetarist's answer is wrong. It is one of the best-established empirical propositions in economics that, for a given level of spending, the amount of money people are willing to hold is greater the lower the interest rate.

After reviewing the research in that field, David Laidler reports:

Of the many experiments that have been performed, only one failed to find a relationship between the demand for money and the rate of interest, and that was carried out by Friedman for the period 1869–1957. . . .

. . . There is an overwhelming body of evidence in favor of the proposition that the demand for money is stably and negatively related to the rate of interest. Of all the issues in monetary economics, this is the one that appears to have been settled most decisively.[31]

31. David E. W. Laidler, *The Demand for Money: Theories and Evidence* (Scranton, Pa.: International Textbook Company, 1969), pp. 96–97. Because these findings disprove the quantity theory of money, a list of the references in the literature is given in the Selected Bibliography on Money and Interest, starting on p. 146.

This checks with both theory and common sense. The interest return on nonmonetary liquid assets—like thrift accounts and marketable securities—is what people and firms sacrifice in holding money, which yields no interest. Thus lower interest rates provide a reduced incentive to economize on cash balances. Since interest rates would have had to be lower to get the same GNP without the tax cut, a larger money supply would have been necessary to do the job. More generally, because of the link between the demand for money and interest, the relationship between money and income cannot be unique. When the tax cut raised take-home pay, people could and would have spent somewhat more even if the Fed had not provided extra cash balances. In that event, interest rates would have had to rise enough to hold the demand for money down to the available supply.

The ticket analogy to money has to be modified in this case. People need cash tickets to buy goods and services, but they hold an inventory of tickets and can make the tickets turn over faster even if the ticket seller refuses to increase his sales. To be sure, the rise in interest rates resulting from the increased scarcity of money would have curtailed—but not eliminated—the economic expansion generated by the tax cut.

In short, the strong economic expansion of 1964–65 would not have taken place in the face of a highly restrictive monetary strategy. Moreover, the job could in principle have been accomplished by a very expansionary monetary strategy without a stimulative fiscal policy. But the rate-oriented monetary policy that was actually pursued would not in itself have quickened the pace of the economy. It supplied a good set of tires for the economy to move on, but fiscal policy was the engine.

The Problems of High Employment

The high-water mark of the economist's prestige in Washington was probably reached late in 1965. At that point, for a brief moment, even congressmen were using the appellation "professor" as a term of respect and approval. There could be no greater tribute to the success of the expansionary policy strategy.

Even under the best of circumstances, with no defense buildup, the attainment of full utilization would have ushered in a new environment with new challenges to economic policy making. In the first place, the growth of output and real incomes was bound to slow down. A significant part of the growth in the 1961–65 period represented a reduction in the initial $50 billion gap between actual and potential output. We were catching up as well as keeping up with productive capacity. Once that catch-up was completed, the growth rate could no longer persistently exceed that of potential—about 4 percent per year. A slowdown in growth from a 5½ to a 4 percent rate had to involve some strain and disappointment. With the extra margin in the rapid 5½ percent advance, the national pie was growing so fast that there was unusually little displeasure about the distribution of the pie among labor and business and other groups. Squabbling about fair shares was bound to intensify once the growth rate slowed down. To paraphrase the travel slogan, half the fun of a full-employment economy is getting there.

Second, once full utilization was attained, the range of tolerance for policy error would have to shrink. Because there had been little risk of excessive demand in the early sixties, any growth performance between 4 and 6 percent could be viewed as qualitatively successful: It would be fast enough to reduce unemployment and not so rapid as to jeopardize essential price stability. Once the economy is close to target, however, there are necessarily dangers from both inadequate and excessive demand. In the earlier period, economists knew what to prescribe, and the medicine worked once the patient was persuaded to take it. But in a healthy, prosperous economy, there was no sure tonic. Like physicians, we can cure pneumonia and look great, but we can't keep our patient from catching cold.

Third, in a world of full utilization, the problem of keeping the economy close to a chosen course is compounded by the uncertainties in choosing the course. The ideal rate of utilization is necessarily a difficult compromise between the objective of maximum production and employment, on the one hand, and the objective of price stability, on the other. We have had little experience historically in confronting that hard choice because the nation has so rarely remained on a reasonably satisfactory growth path. Except during wartime inflations, we have not been at full employment long enough to test, under these circumstances, the supply capabilities of the economy, its price-cost performance, or public attitudes toward price increases of various rates.

In 1965 the nation was entering essentially uncharted territory. The economists in government were ready to meet the welcome problems of prosperity. But they recognized that they could not provide a good encore to their success in achieving high-level employment. As Gardner Ackley put the problem in a talk delivered during December 1965:

. . . The plain fact is that economists simply don't know as much as we would like to know about the terms of trade between price increases and employment gains. We would all like the economy to tread the narrow path of a balanced, parallel growth of demand and capacity—at as high a level of capacity utilization as is consistent with reasonable price stability, and without creating imbalances that would make continuing advance unsustainable. But the macroeconomics of a high employment economy is insufficiently known to allow us to map that path with a high degree of reliability. . . .

. . . It is easy to prescribe expansionary policies in a period of slack. Managing high-level prosperity is a vastly more difficult business and requires vastly superior knowledge. The prestige that our profession has built up in the Government and around the country in recent years could suffer if economists give incorrect policy advice based on inadequate knowledge. We need to improve that knowledge.[32]

32. Gardner Ackley, "The Contribution of Economists to Policy Formation," *Journal of Finance,* Vol. 21 (May 1966), pp. 174 and 176.

chapter three

The Challenges of Defense and High Employment

As matters developed, the normal challenges of high employment became immensely complicated by the upsurge in defense spending. On July 28, 1965, President Johnson requested additional funds for Vietnam and announced that a further supplemental appropriation would be required in January 1966. That opened a new chapter in the economic expansion. We entered a world of rapidly growing defense spending at a time when we were approaching full utilization of resources. For the next three years, the upward movement of the defense budget exerted a key influence on fiscal policy and on economic activity.

The Complications of Defense

The shadows of the defense budget also obscured our view of the workings of our economy in a sustained high-employment situation. The profession had many unanswered questions about how private demand and public policy would perform during an extended period of prosperity. Economists were hoping to determine from experience the feasibility of a combination of 4 percent unemployment and a 2 percent rate of price increase. But the defense spurt ruined that experiment. Economists hoped to find that private spending would display increased stability in sustained prosperity, but private demand was buffeted by shifting fiscal and monetary winds. Hence many of the key questions about a peacetime high-employment environment remain unanswered. Those answers simply cannot be read from our recent record without a careful allowance for the major impact of the defense buildup. Vietnam plays the Danish prince in the *Hamlet* of recent economic history.

A significant rise in defense outlays necessarily creates problems of economic stabilization and allocation. If fiscal policy is initially on track, an unanticipated increase in defense outlays pulls it off the track. Fiscal policy is made too stimulative and aggregate demand excessive, unless the government takes neutralizing actions. In principle, such actions can take the form of (a) higher taxes to mop up private purchasing power and curtail the total of consumer and business spending; (b) reduced outlays on government nondefense programs; or (c) a more restrictive monetary policy to curb private outlays.

The proper neutralizing dosage—*how much* restraint—depends upon the magnitude and timing of the extra defense outlays. It also depends upon the impact of extra defense on private psychology; in principle, private spending in relation to income may be either encouraged or discouraged and, in practice, the effects may be extremely hard to assess. The proper choice among the various instruments of policy—*what kind* of restraint—depends, however, primarily on social priorities about allocation rather than on stabilization considerations. To be sure, the stabilization effectiveness of various tools may not be identical. Some instruments may be more reliable and have more readily predictable effects than others and hence may be more likely to keep the economy close to the desired path. There may, in some instances, be a premium on curbing certain categories of civilian demand in order to avoid bottlenecks in particular types of labor, materials, or industrial capacity.

But these considerations are generally secondary to the big social question: What types of spending should be squeezed in order to make room for the resources claimed by defense? It is tempting to suggest that the required cutbacks be confined to the federal nondefense sector. Life would then be simple: Taxes need not be changed and the national balance between the public and the private sectors need not be disturbed. But, on any reasonable interpretation of social preferences, acquiring guns at the expense solely—or even primarily—of public sector butter is a grossly irrational trade. Such a decision would make sense only if all the lowest priority items in the entire national shopping list were in the 12 percent of our gross national product (GNP) devoted to federal nondefense outlays. Would anyone care to argue that case?

A substantial volume of federal nondefense outlays, including interest on the public debt and social insurance payments, is required to fulfill contractual commitments. Other federal outlays—like those for the Federal Bureau of Investigation and Internal Revenue Service—fulfill national housekeeping needs that lose no urgency in a defense emergency. Another substantial area of federal spending is aimed at the problems of the poor and the cities. To concentrate the squeeze there is to decide that the poor and the cities should pay most heavily for the war.

The overhead cost to society of more guns might sensibly be imposed proportionately on private butter and public butter. Most would then fall on private spending just because it is so big. Federal nondefense outlays would carry a 12 or, at most, 15 percent share of the restraint.

Either higher taxes or additional monetary restraint can be used to make private butter share the burden. Of the two, taxes get the higher grade on allocation grounds. A hike in corporate and individual income taxes will have an essentially across-the-board impact in curbing various types of private spending. Monetary restraint, on the other hand, bears down on those sectors that are most dependent on credit financing, like home-building, business investment, and consumer durables. There is no obvious premium on restraining these sectors and hence no persuasive case for a particularly restrictive monetary policy during a defense mobilization.[1]

All of this adds up to a straightforward recipe for dealing with the problem of war finance. Take a substantial rise in taxes

1. It can be argued that investment expenditures should be squeezed relatively more severely during wartime and allowed to rise more rapidly in the postwar years, thus spreading the consumption sacrifice more evenly over a longer period, including war and postwar years. On the other hand, a case can be made that, in view of the special needs of defense industries and the general premium on plant capacity, private investment expenditures deserve a particularly high priority in wartime. In my judgment, the battle between these two sides is a draw.

and a small cutback in federal nondefense outlays so that, in combination, overall fiscal policy remains about as stimulative as it would have been in the absence of the additional defense spending. Since the stimulus of defense will then be neutralized within the framework of fiscal policy, monetary policy can be left essentially unaltered—whether viewed in terms of interest rates and credit conditions or in terms of the growth of money and other credit flows. If we knew we were about to fight a war costing, say, 3 percent of our GNP, and if we applied this recipe, the resulting problems of resource allocation and stabilization would not have to be overwhelming.

One major difficulty is that we never know how big a war we are about to fight. Decisions on manpower and procurement for defense are made sequentially, and each new important decision creates new economic problems. If the defense budget is scaled up by new military decisions, a further neutralizing stabilization move is required. The tax dog may have to keep chasing the defense rabbit and may not be able to keep up. During the Korean war, we were willing to pursue the rabbit diligently: Three major pieces of tax-raising legislation were enacted in 1950 and 1951. But there are inevitable legislative and economic lags, as well as substantial costs in changing tax rates frequently. Monetary restraint can help to offset some small markups in defense outlays and can help to reduce the uncertainties and urgency of frequent changes in tax rates.

Economic policy is thus inevitably handicapped in a period of defense mobilization. If a war turns out to be larger and to last longer than is initially anticipated, the neutralizing actions are bound to lag behind. Thus an inflationary bias in wartime may be an inescapable consequence of preserving the flexibility of our military responses. This fact of life is not an argument for rigid defense budgeting. Nor does it help us to decide whether a war is worth fighting. If a conflict is worth the sacrifice of American blood, it is worth the sacrifice of several points on the price index. And if it isn't worth the sacrifice of blood. that in itself should be decisive without regard to the economic implications.

While wars are thus bound to be destabilizing to the economy, the Vietnam war turned out to be more disruptive than was necessary. To see why this was the case, one must review the history of the period.

The Economic Spurt of Late 1965

Part of the disruption occurred because the initial impact of defense spending on aggregate demand far exceeded expectations. The annual rate of defense purchases rose abruptly by $3.3 billion from the second to the fourth quarter of 1965. In addition, defense orders jumped and swelled business inventories of matériel. Economic activity zoomed from mid-1965 into early 1966, as shown in Figure 4. In the fourth quarter, GNP rose by the largest amount in history. Unemployment fell to 4.0 percent of the labor force by year-end. This leap exceeded anyone's expectations or desires. It made an inflationary spurt inevitable for 1966, even though prices did not accelerate sharply at first.

The initial burst of price and wage pressures occurred in raw materials, and in services and other unorganized labor-intensive, low-wage sectors. These highly competitive areas are normally characterized by flexible prices and wages, and it is no surprise that they led the march to inflation. The facts clearly refute any theory that would blame monopolistic firms and big unions for the initial deterioration of our price performance. Market pressures—not monopoly power—made the difference between the good price record of the early sixties and its deterioration in 1966.

Consumer spending and residential construction behaved normally late in 1965, but business investment in plant and equipment skyrocketed. Capital spending had been rising at a brisk rate for two years, and some further expansion had been planned by businessmen for the second half of 1965, according to the periodic survey conducted by the Department of Commerce and the Securities and Exchange Commission. These plans were revised upward substantially: Actual outlays during

Figure 4. *Increases in Output and Prices, Selected Periods, 1963–69*
(Percentage increase expressed at annual rates)

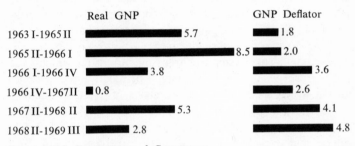

	Real GNP	GNP Deflator
1963 I-1965 II	5.7	1.8
1965 II-1966 I	8.5	2.0
1966 I-1966 IV	3.8	3.6
1966 IV-1967 II	0.8	2.6
1967 II-1968 II	5.3	4.1
1968 II-1969 III	2.8	4.8

Source: U.S. Department of Commerce.

the fourth quarter were 5 percent higher than the plans reported in July, marking one of the largest upward revisions in the post-Korean experience of the survey. Some acceleration was to be expected in response to the general strength of final demand and the direct impact of increased defense procurement. But even in retrospect, statistical approaches generally underestimate the capital expenditures of this period.

Surely, financial conditions did not spur the boom, although they permitted it to be financed. No businessman found it cheaper or easier to get credit in the second half of 1965 than previously. On the contrary, monetary policy became somewhat less accommodative. As strong demands for expenditures triggered large increases in demands for funds, the Fed held back on supplying part of the credit demanded and interest rates began to move upward. The explanation of the capital goods boom must lie in the effect of the defense buildup on business expectations. In the view of the American businessman, the initial increments to the defense budget virtually eliminated any danger of recession or sluggish growth in 1966. A high floor was established under the economy, and the downside risks essentially disappeared.

Economists cannot feel proud of their diagnostic or predictive performance during the second half of 1965. To be sure, no one could have foreseen the upsurge before the Vietnam supplemental budget was announced. It is neither surprising nor embarrassing that the profession was, to the best of my knowledge, unanimous as of midyear that the second half of 1965 would witness moderation from the brisk advance of the first half. What is disappointing, however, is that we took so long to recognize the full significance of emerging developments.

Our intelligence system for tracking current movements did not perform well. This was the only period in my experience during which the preliminary estimates of economic activity qualitatively misrepresented the true situation. As of November 1965, official estimates of GNP showed a rise of $36 billion and a real growth rate of 5½ percent for the first three quarters of the year—essentially a continuation of the brisk growth of 1964. The estimates today for that same period show a gain of $46 billion and an enormous 8 percent rate of real growth. In retrospect, I regret that we did not pay more attention to the strong bullish signals registered by indicators of business credit demand; perhaps they could and should have been read as foreshadowing a boom in investment.

The financial press seemed especially bearish, expressing great concern for the vigor of the old expansion. In September, when Gardner Ackley stated that the economy had plenty of steam and was capable of generating a $40 billion increase in GNP during 1966, his statement was challenged as overly bullish.[2] The initial round of forecasts by business economists for 1966 was characterized as a "jet model"—it pointed to a GNP of $707 billion. Our latest estimates of 1966 GNP show a $65 billion gain for the year and have topped even the 747 jumbo jet model.

The general recognition that the economy was booming can be pinpointed to the release of the Commerce-SEC survey of plant and equipment spending early in December 1965. At that juncture, it became clear that the makers of fiscal and monetary

2. See, for example, "The Pitfalls of Prosperity," editorial, *New York Times,* Sept. 11, 1965.

policy faced a new assignment of restraining the economy, and, indeed, that restrictive steps should have been taken earlier.

The Turn in Monetary Policy

On December 5, 1965, the Federal Reserve raised its discount rate, signaling a turn of monetary policy toward restraint. This momentous action marked the first time during the sixties that the Fed tightened for the purpose of curbing aggregate demand, and even more significantly, the only important disagreement between the administration and the Federal Reserve during the Kennedy and Johnson years. President Johnson promptly expressed his regret about the Board's decision: "My view and the view of the Secretary of the Treasury and the Council of Economic Advisers is that the decision on interest rates should be a coordinated policy decision in January, when the nature and impact of the administration's budgetary and Viet-Nam decisions are known." [3]

One aspect of the Federal Reserve's action was the verdict that the time had come to apply economic restraint. To administration economists, this seemed debatable at the time the decision was being made by the Fed; but, once the plant and equipment survey was in front of them, they recognized that the Fed was right on that score.

There was, however, another issue, which remains complicated even in retrospect. That issue concerned the strategy for devising an adequate and properly composed mix of fiscal and monetary restraint. Six weeks before the fiscal 1967 budget was to be sent to the Congress, it seemed important to administration officials to have all the options open on both fiscal and monetary policy. So long as the Federal Reserve held its fire, it was possible to conceive of a program of fiscal restraint which might be explicitly tailored to avoid any need for tight money and, indeed, might be presented to the Congress and

---

3. *Public Papers of the Presidents of the United States: Lyndon B. Johnson, 1965* (1966), Vol. 2, p. 1137.

the nation as an alternative to monetary restraint. Once the discount rate was raised, tight money appeared inevitable and irreversible. Many of us in the administration thus felt at the time that the timing of the Federal Reserve move had impaired the chances of rational and adequate fiscal actions for the January 1966 budget program. In retrospect, however, overwhelming political pressures dominated the fiscal program and I cannot honestly claim that a different posture by the Federal Reserve would have made the difference.

Fortunately, both sides reacted constructively to this disagreement. There was genuine regret and a mutual sense of responsibility for the failure in communication—the administration had not fully comprehended the Federal Reserve's anxiety about developments in financial markets, nor had the Fed fully understood the problems faced by administration officials engaged in fiscal planning. The result was a determination on both sides to improve coordination. Regular luncheons of the members of the Council of Economic Advisers and the Governors of the Federal Reserve were established early in 1966, and this symbolic action was one part of a successful effort to increase the flow of information and the exchange of views between fiscal planners and monetary policy makers.

Fiscal Decision Making

The key fiscal decision for the January 1966 budget program was a negative one: A general tax increase was not proposed. The defense program incorporated in the January budget pointed significantly upward, although it later proved to underestimate the magnitude of the escalation by a wide margin. Given these budget estimates, the President was told by his economic advisers at the end of 1965 that a general increase in income taxes was desirable to avoid excess demand. The President did propose—and Congress promptly enacted—a significant but clearly inadequate bits-and-pieces revenue package which rescinded excise tax cuts, instituted graduated withholding on individual income taxes, and accelerated the collection of corporate income taxes. Meanwhile, the general tax increase was placed on the back burner with warnings by the President in his economic report and his budget message that it might have to be recommended later during the course of 1966.

President Johnson stated publicly in 1968 that he had not proposed a general tax increase at that time because "it was evident that it would be impossible to get a tax increase in 1966." He elaborated on this in a speech to the Business Council in December 1968: "We knew we needed action on taxes in 1966. Many of you in this room will remember what happened when, in the month of March 1966, I asked how much support you would give me. Not a hand went up. And I was told that I could get but four votes in the Tax Committee of the Congress out of 25." [4]

This political reality should be clear in retrospect, especially in view of the antagonism to the surcharge proposal in 1967–68. There was much less reason for higher taxes to get a sympathetic hearing at the beginning of 1966. At that time, to the untrained eye, the economy seemed to be doing remarkably well. Anybody who wanted to slow things down was a killjoy. All the favorable consequences of the boom were clear: Profits were soaring; consumer living standards were improving dramatically; poverty was declining sharply; and the promised land of 4 percent unemployment was finally being reached. On the other hand, there was no compelling evidence of acceleration in prices and wages, deterioration of the balance of payments, skyrocketing of interest rates, or acute pressures in financial markets. All these unfavorable consequences of the boom were still forecasts rather than facts.

The economists in the administration watched with pain and frustration as fiscal policy veered off course. The new developments meant they were no longer calling the shots in fiscal policy. The January 1966 budget marked the first defeat of the new economics by the old politics since Kennedy's decision in

4. *Weekly Compilation of Presidential Documents,* Vol. 4, p. 617 and pp. 1670–71.

August 1962 to delay a tax-cut recommendation.[5] Even more important, the new economics could not pass its crucial test because of the defense upsurge and the political paralysis of tax rates. The new economists had insisted repeatedly to their critics that the policy of fiscal stimulus would be turned off in time and would be amended to head off inflation when the economy did reach full employment. For political—not economic—reasons, the skeptics won the debate.

Postmortems of the 1966 tax decision still make an interesting parlor game. Even though a presidential recommendation for a tax hike would not have been enacted in 1966, might it have paved the way for an earlier victory in 1967? Would a fiscal program on the side of virtue proposed by the President have redounded to his prestige—and incidentally to that of his economists—even if it had been rejected by the Congress? Or would the revelation that the President could not implement an urgent economic program have harmed his image and have shaken the confidence of the business and financial community? Would a presidential recommendation for a tax increase have seriously impaired the Great Society legislative program for 1966 and, indeed, was that an important reason why the President decided not to undertake the crusade? Such questions are great fun, despite the fact that we can't answer them—maybe, indeed, because we can't answer them.

Neither can we be sure exactly how the economy would have responded if a tax hike had in fact been enacted early in 1966. But it is reasonable to believe that tax action could have prevented a heavy burden from falling upon monetary policy and could have helped to check inflation. Still, it would not have performed all the miracles that are sometimes claimed.[6] Enormous faith is occasionally displayed in the tax action that wasn't taken. No actual measure of economic policy has been nearly

5. "Radio and Television Report to the American People on the State of the National Economy, August 13, 1962," *Public Papers of the Presidents of the United States: John F. Kennedy, 1962* (1963), p. 616.
6. See, for example, Edwin L. Dale, Jr., "The Inflation Goof," *New Republic* (Jan. 4, 1969), pp. 16–17.

that effective. In the postmortem of 1966, three important limitations must be borne in mind. First, a good deal of inflationary tinder had been ignited in the second half of 1965, and it would have burned during much of 1966 even if appropriate fiscal actions had been undertaken early in the year. Second, a tax increase of the right size to neutralize the defense stimulus envisioned in the budget program—and to avoid the need for tight money—would clearly have been inadequate for the actual level of defense spending, which topped the budget by $10 billion. Third, even with the inaction on taxes in 1966, the nation had an excellent second chance to get on the track of noninflationary prosperity in 1967.

Defense Estimates

Undoubtedly, if the level of defense outlays for fiscal 1967 had been accurately foreseen by the administration in January 1966, the case for offsetting fiscal restraining action would have been much more evident. The underestimate of $10 billion may have been an important cause of the political paralysis on taxes. In retrospect it is clear that every dimension of the Vietnam war was underestimated at that time, and it is hardly surprising that the volume of defense expenditures was projected too low.

The $10 billion underestimate had two distinct parts: (1) the inaccurate translation of the assumed defense program into a dollar estimate of expenditures; and (2) the impact on outlays of decisions made after January 1966 that added to the size and duration of the military effort in Vietnam. The second was by far the larger source of the divergence. The budget assumed that hostilities would end within fiscal 1967 and that provision need not be made for their continuation beyond June 30, 1967. According to subsequent estimates made by the staff of the Defense Department, about $5 billion of the overshoot in military outlays can be directly attributed to the breakdown of that assumption. Indeed, by the beginning of the 1967 fiscal year, commitments and expenditures were being made to provide for the contingency of a longer war. Of the remaining $5 billion, at

least half was the result of other program decisions after
January 1966 that involved a step-up in Vietnam activity during
the fiscal year. The underestimate of the cost of the initial program amounted to about $2 billion. To be sure, that represents
a significant imperfection in the staff capabilities of the government in tracing out the economic impact of its own activities.
But it was not the big problem.

The defense establishment implemented decisions to step up
activity with remarkable speed. Although large and bureaucratic, the Pentagon was light on its feet, translating new decisions promptly into increased outlays. The resulting shifts had
larger and more disruptive economic effects than any surprises
encountered in components of private demand during the sixties. The defense estimates had to be scaled up again and again
because the Vietnam conflict turned into a much larger, longer,
and more serious war than had been anticipated. Historians
face a major task in explaining why we thought the tail we
were grabbing belonged to a mouse when in fact it was that of
a bear. But that question transcends budget arithmetic and fiscal economics.

I should note, however, one institutional feature that may
bias estimates of defense spending in a downward direction
during a period of rising expenditures. The top management of
the Defense Department is likely to be pushing outlays downward by curbing commitments and orders and pruning out non-
essential procurement. The officials in lower echelons are pushing upward in order to acquire plenty of men and matériel to
handle their military assignments. The overall budgetary estimates are approved at the top and they become tools of control
as well as forecasts, serving as allocations to those responsible
for procurement. The Secretary is more concerned about setting
a good target than making a good forecast—much like a
graduate student who is really convincing himself when he tells
you how soon he will complete his dissertation. The effort to
restrain the subordinates is not likely to be totally successful.
Hence this process yields an imperfect projection of defense outlays; yet it keeps actual military spending lower than it would
be if the process of estimating were unbiased.

Search for the Second Best

The principles of fiscal policy prescribe higher taxes as the best antidote to the stimulative force of extra defense spending. They do not tell us what to do if that prescription cannot be filled. In 1966, the search for second-best alternatives yielded results, but some of the remedies were not very strong and others had undesirable side effects.

To relax and accept inflation was obviously not a satisfactory alternative on either domestic or international grounds. Mandatory controls on prices and wages were also clearly a most undesirable way of dealing with inflation. Throughout the Vietnam period, yards of copy in the press have been devoted to rumors of price and wage controls. These stories were unmitigated fiction—controls were never seriously contemplated in the Johnson administration. Rumors of impending controls were particularly rife in the fall of 1966; according to the alleged scenario, they were to be slapped on by presidential order right after the congressional elections. When I said in October 1966 that "there is no earthly reason why we should want to or need to travel that route," [7] I was credited with buoying up the stock market—along with Secretary of Commerce John T. Connor, who made the same point that day. The rumors kept popping up, and government officials kept trying to shoot them down. In its 1968 report, the Council tried to express its distaste in tones that would come through loud and clear:

. . . Mandatory controls on prices and wages . . . distort resource allocation; they require reliance either on necessarily clumsy and arbitrary rules or the inevitably imperfect decisions of Government officials; they offer countless temptations to evasion or violation; they require a vast administrative apparatus. All these reasons make them repugnant.[8]

7. "National Defense and Prosperity" (remarks before the American Ordnance Association, Fort Lesley J. McNair, Washington, D.C., Oct. 12, 1966; processed), p. 13.

8. *Economic Report of the President together with the Annual Report of the Council of Economic Advisers, February 1968,* p. 119. Hereafter, this document will be referred to as *Economic Report* or *Annual Report of the CEA,* followed by the year.

As one way to battle against inflation, the government did significantly step up its jawbone efforts to talk down wages and prices in areas of market power. To a large extent this activity took the form of "private communications and meetings between Government officials and leaders of business and labor designed to . . . solicit . . . cooperation. . . ." [9] In a great many specific instances, the Council asked firms to exercise restraint in price decisions, including requests for rollbacks of increases already announced. Businessmen were also informed that the administration appreciated a willingness on their part to discuss in advance any price changes that they were contemplating. On several occasions, the Council issued public statements criticizing certain private decisions on prices and wages. In January 1967, the Council noted some successes:

> The outcome of these activities cannot be fully known. In a number of cases, it is clear that price increases which were announced or contemplated have been rescinded, reduced in amount or coverage, or delayed. Some companies have indicated that their subsequent price decisions were affected even where their decision in the immediate case was not changed.[10]

Similarly favorable responses by labor leaders in wage decisions could not be reported, but the moral suasion efforts did seem to have considerable effect in stiffening the resistance of management to large wage demands. The efforts on wages and prices were necessarily asymmetrical, since it takes two to sign a wage bargain and only one to make a price decision.

The nature of the appeals for restraint had to be modified in the light of market realities. Once food and service prices began to accelerate, it became patently unrealistic to ask organized labor to accept wage increases that merely paralleled the trend growth of productivity, in line with the earlier Kennedy-Johnson guideposts. By the end of 1966, such settlements would have barely covered the year's increase in consumer prices, thus providing no rise in real income. Some of the rise in the cost of living had to be reflected in wage gains; but, so long as a full esca-

9. *Annual Report of the CEA, 1967,* p. 126.
10. *Ibid.,* p. 127.

lation was prevented, the wage-price spiral would be moderated.

The Council reports in 1967 and 1968 stressed this objective, substituting temporarily for the productivity guide an interim qualitative standard of partial adjustment of negotiated wages to the cost of living. Similarly, once labor and material costs rose, management could not be asked to absorb these increases without adjusting prices to some degree. The Council stressed the need for partial absorption in its plea for restraint in pricing.[11]

Special problems arose in concentrated industries with high operating rates, as oligopolistic prices moved up toward pure monopoly prices. In general, excess capacity of competitors acts as an important disciplinary force on pricing in oligopoly. When excess capacity diminishes, any firm contemplating a price hike incurs less risk of losing its share of the market. Competitors are more likely to follow—rather than to contest—price increases because they are less able to expand output to serve more of the market. The demand curve facing each individual oligopolist thus becomes less elastic at high operating rates, and the effective degree of monopoly in the industry is increased. For this reason, oligopoly creates a tendency toward *rising* prices as well as higher levels of prices in a prosperous economy; the phenomenon was empirically evident in 1966.[12]

In all these ways, concentrated industries and large unions are bound to climb aboard an inflationary bandwagon, even when they don't start it rolling. Voluntary cooperation can, in principle, ameliorate the decisions of big business and big labor and thereby moderate the pace of inflation.

While the appeals of the administration could and did make some difference in the nation's price and wage performance, the tides of excess demand could not be talked down. Because of

11. *Annual Report of the CEA, 1967,* pp. 128–32, and . . . *1968,* pp. 125–26.

12. See Gardner Ackley, "The Contribution of Guidelines," in George P. Shultz and Robert Z. Aliber (eds.), *Guidelines, Informal Controls, and the Market Place: Policy Choices in a Full Employment Economy* (University of Chicago Press. 1966). pp. 67–78. esp. p. 71.

the resulting appearance of failure, the guideposts were badly splintered in the eyes of the American public.

The efforts at moral suasion, moreover, placed government in an adversary position with respect to business and labor. Looking at his own situation, nearly every businessman and labor leader could convince himself that he was really behind in the wage-price race and was trying merely to get justice for his stockholders or his members. Yet, from a public point of view, many of the price and wage decisions did speed up the spiral and hence were unpatriotic in their effects, if not in their motivation. The Council of Economic Advisers served as the government's chief policeman in the resulting confrontations because, quite understandably, neither the Secretary of Labor nor the Secretary of Commerce felt that he could be publicly critical of price and wage decisions without compromising his effectiveness with private groups in other key areas. But the Council was not particularly well equipped for this task, and its professional image was tarnished by performing it.

Finally, turning the spotlight on guidepost efforts ran some risk of distracting attention from the main cause of the inflation, namely, the excess demand created by an inappropriate fiscal policy. Within the administration, there were no illusions: It was clearly recognized that the public budget and not private action was the engine of inflation. Elsewhere, however, the guideposts seemed to have some overly enthusiastic supporters who viewed them as a substitute for fiscal restraint.

The use of the jawbone in 1966–68 had many drawbacks. But, in a period of acute shortage of good anti-inflationary tools, it did help, in my judgment, to slow both the spiral and the spread of inflationary expectations.

Another stabilization weapon of limited potency was the repeated but careful curtailment of the nondefense budget. The federal civilian program in the January 1966 budget and every budget thereafter was a good deal lower than it would have been in the absence of the Vietnam war. Though it moved along a rising trend, nondefense spending grew more moderately than would have been desirable and possible had it not been for the military emergency. To be sure, major increases in social security programs took effect during the Vietnam period —most notably the initiation of Medicare. But these were financed by additional taxes adopted for the express purpose, and they did not contribute to the inappropriate fiscal stimulus of the era. Apart from social security and higher interest costs on the federal debt, other nondefense outlays rose by $19 billion from mid-1965 to mid-1969. Along a noninflationary, high-employment growth track, with no changes in tax rates, federal revenues (excluding social insurance taxes) would have risen well over $30 billion during that period. Thus federal nondefense expenditures were held well within the bounds that would have been feasible if defense spending had continued on a plateau.

The squeeze on civilian programs was felt in every budget; it was particularly evident in cutbacks announced out of budget-making season. Explicit packages to trim non-Vietnam spending were set forth in the fall of 1966, again in the fall of 1967, and then in the spring of 1968 in conjunction with the enactment of the tax increase. Still the administration supported a considerable initiation and expansion of those domestic social programs which stood at the very top of the President's priority list. Programs which had been launched in 1964 and 1965 and those that were newly proposed during the Vietnam period were designed to meet urgent needs on the home front and were particularly aimed at aiding the poor and improving the environment of the cities. In retrospect and in perspective, there should be no regrets that these efforts were not squeezed to a greater extent for anti-inflationary purposes.

Reliance on Tight Money

With only a little help from other policies, the monetary authorities shouldered most of the thankless burden of restraining the booming economy in 1966. The availability of reserves to banks was sharply curtailed at the start of the year, and interest rates moved upward as the demand for credit outstripped supplies provided by the Federal Reserve. Credit flows continued to be large in the early months of 1966, and the money supply rose rapidly in the first four months of the year. Yet housing starts began to fall at the start of 1966, and by April they were at their lowest rate in three years. As the monetary authorities continued deliberately and gradually to tighten the screws, credit flows did fall off markedly during the spring and summer, and the squeeze extended to areas other than home mortgages.

Still the major impact of tight money fell on homebuilding; outlays for·residential structures declined sharply—nearly $6 billion (annual rate) from the fourth quarter of 1965 to the fourth quarter of 1966. Starts nosedived even more dramatically from an annual rate of 1.5 million units in the former period to 0.9 million in the latter.

Studies of the influence of the 1966 money squeeze on business capital spending and inventory investment reveal only a relatively small impact.[13] Nor has anyone found dramatic effects on outlays for consumer durables as a result of the reduced availability and higher cost of installment credit. Tight money may, however, have contributed to the marked weakening of consumer spending in relation to income that developed late in 1966. This shift in behavior remains a puzzle. It may have reflected, at least in part, the reduced value of household assets, as both common stocks and bonds dropped sharply in price during the monetary squeeze.

Even on conservative assumptions, tight money had a remarkably impressive total effect. As the Council reported its assessment, the impact was as large as one would have expected from a 10 percent surcharge on corporate and individual income tax liabilities.[14] But unlike the results of such a hike in income taxes, the impact of monetary policy was terribly lopsided—even more so than had been expected. In that respect, tight money worked like a fiscal action pinpointed to finance defense through a substantial excise tax on the purchase of new

13. Jean Crockett, Irwin Friend, and Henry Shavell, "The Impact of Monetary Stringency on Business Investment," *Survey of Current Business,* Vol. 47 (August 1967), pp. 10–27.

14. *Annual Report of the CEA, 1967,* p. 60.

homes. That type of tax program would have been hooted off Capitol Hill for its obvious inequity and illogic.

It was hardly surprising that, on similar grounds, a strong political outcry arose against tight money. The Council shared the Federal Reserve's judgment that rising interest rates were a lesser evil than rising prices; that curbing aggregate demand through a heavy and uneven burden on homebuilding was not so bad as tolerating a runaway economy, and that creating uncertainties and anxieties in credit markets was less serious than providing the financial fuel for a dangerous inflationary boom.

In this episode, the Federal Reserve's independence proved to be a valuable national asset. It permitted the President and his administration to assume a passive role, tolerating an unpopular tight money policy silently without explicitly approving or endorsing it. The Council's job was to make sure that the administration did not impede the Fed in the execution of its unpleasant assignment. President Johnson was a populist at heart and found it very hard to believe that escalating interest rates were a lesser evil than anything else. But he understood the problem and let his head rule his heart. When former President Truman issued a public blast at the Federal Reserve in the summer of 1966, President Johnson responded very mildly, agreeing simply that "we need to find better ways to restrain inflationary pressures than by resorting merely to the high interest rates we have been witnessing." [15]

The Federal Reserve probed, tested, and reacted. It shot in the dark in some instances. Yet the Board put on an outstanding performance in 1966, making wise judgments and, most of all, having the courage to act promptly and decisively on them. The objectives could not have been carried out if the Board had been frozen by timidity or hogtied by rigid rules about the growth of the money supply, the level of interest rates, or any other criterion of monetary policy. With perfect hindsight, one might conclude that the Fed had a little margin to spare and

---

15. *Public Papers of the Presidents of the United States: Lyndon B. Johnson, 1966* (1967), Vol. 2, p. 934.

could have been somewhat less tight at the peak of the summer. Such hindsight judgments are analogous to criticisms of an alert driver who has just avoided a jaywalking child because he careened to a halt when he still had three or four feet to spare.

When financial pressures mounted to ever greater heights during the summer of 1966, the administration brought fiscal policy back into the ball game with the suspension of the investment tax credit, the only tax measure that was reported to be legislatively feasible at that time. This proposal had been under serious consideration ever since the plant and equipment survey in March revealed the tremendous strength of business investment demand. While the Congress seemed willing to take such action and no other tax action, the administration was strongly committed to the investment credit as a highly desirable long-term structural feature of our tax system. It was also concerned about the thorny housekeeping problems of a temporary suspension.

When, however, the midsummer survey of plant and equipment spending indicated further advances, and when capital markets continued to be jolted by strong demands to finance these outlays, the President decided to recommend temporary suspension. That proposal was the kingpin of the "little budget" that the President sent to Congress on September 8, 1966, which also included cutbacks in nondefense expenditures and in the scheduled issues of federal agency securities. It was no coincidence that interest rates turned down sharply during September from their peaks of 1966. To the financial markets, the little budget demonstrated that fiscal policy was coming off the bench and could be expected to join monetary policy in providing restraint.

The Welcome Slowdown

Once the brakes worked, they took hold rather abruptly. Because of the nosedive in homebuilding and the weakening of consumer buying, final demand slacked off in the closing months of 1966. When business production schedules were not scaled down correspondingly, inventories piled up. By the beginning of

1967, the boom was no longer a threat. Rather the danger became that of going into a tailspin. Monetary policy had been reversed toward ease late in 1966, and its support of economic activity continued to be appropriate early in 1967.

When the plant and equipment survey in March 1967 showed that the capital boom was over, it became safe to restore the investment tax credit. It had always been recognized that the investment credit could not follow the scenario of the 1966 statute, suspended throughout 1967 and reinstated at the beginning of 1968; such a schedule would have produced a famine in orders for capital goods late in 1967 by offering an irresistible incentive for businessmen to wait a few months. Hence it was necessary for the administration to decide fairly early in 1967 whether to reinstate the credit sooner or to keep it inactive longer. The end of the capital spending boom made the decision rather easy.

Even with the weak overall economic outlook immediately on the horizon at the start of 1967, it seemed likely that the economy would once again need restraint later in the year because of continued increases in defense spending and the gradual working off of the inventory imbalance. With that requirement in view, the January 1967 budget called for a 6 percent tax surcharge on individual and corporate income taxes to take effect later in the year. A specific effective date was necessary for budget-estimating purposes, and July 1 was selected, although there was considerable uncertainty about just when a tax increase would be appropriate.

The policy strategy was designed essentially to replay the 1966 hand and to do it right the second time. Politically, a tax increase seemed considerably more feasible in 1967, because of the experiences of 1966, which had underlined the costs of inflation and the distortions involved in using monetary brakes to offset a fiscal accelerator. Yet restrictive tax action could not be taken until the immediate economic slowdown had been surmounted and a rebound was visible to the congressional eye. This strategy of shifting the fiscal-monetary mix depended upon accurate forecasting and appropriate timing of policy measures. The existing slowdown permitted the monetary brakes to be released without an imminent threat of inflation. Then it was necessary for the economy to get back on its feet and show vigor. Finally, it was essential that the fiscal stimulus be curbed by the timely enactment of a substantial tax increase.

As matters developed, the strategy earned a top grade in economics and a failing mark in politics. It was a vintage year for many economic forecasters who relied on a Keynesian income-expenditure approach. As projected, the first half of 1967 did turn out to be sluggish. Dominated by an inventory adjustment, the economy paused much as it had during earlier periods of expansion in 1951–52 and 1956, but the recession predicted by a few non-Keynesian forecasters was clearly avoided. The unemployment rate stayed around 4 percent. Also as predicted, the slowdown—and the accompanying monetary ease—generated considerable benefits: A decline in interest rates, a rebound in housing, and distinct and definite relief in price advances. After rising at a rate of 4 percent during much of 1966, consumer prices increased at a rate of less than 2½ percent in the first half of 1967. Wholesale industrial prices remained on a plateau after the summer of 1966, helped by a downward correction in prices of raw materials.

The Second Chance

The rebound at midyear was also remarkably true to the script that the economic forecasters had written at the start of 1967. As the Council had projected in January:

By midyear, construction should be recovering with the stimulus of monetary ease; and inventory investment should be leveling off at a moderate rate. In combination, these two sectors should significantly strengthen over-all private demand. A shift toward restraint in fiscal policy is appropriate at that time to assure that demand does not outrun capacity, that movement toward restoration of price stability is maintained, and that monetary policy does not have to be tightened again.[16]

When a Troika review of the economy in July concluded that this forecast had been realized, the President's economic

16. *Annual Report of the CEA, 1967,* p. 62.

and financial advisers unanimously recommended that he press his request for higher taxes on the basis of the evidence then at hand. Largely because defense estimates had been marked up again, the surcharge proposal was scaled up to 10 percent. At this point, the nation had an excellent second chance to get on the path of noninflationary prosperity. That chance depended upon prompt congressional enactment of the tax increase, and the entire strategy failed when legislative action did not take place.

The Federal Reserve and the administration might have chosen an alternative stabilization strategy that would not have risked a congressional rebuff. It would have involved continued reliance on monetary brakes to offset the budgetary accelerator. Some easing of credit might still have been appropriate early in 1967, but only a little. Monetary restraint could have been assisted by an extension of the suspension of the investment credit rather than its early reinstatement. If overall economic activity and the price level had been the only targets of stabilization policy, such a strategy would have been very attractive. Monetary policy had demonstrably curbed inflation in 1966 and there was every reason to believe that it could do so again in 1967 and 1968. But interest rates—as well as prices—were social targets and so was the composition of the restraint among industries and economic groups. A stabilization policy that continued to kick homebuilding while it was down and that once again put enormous pressure on financial markets would not have met social priorities, even if it made prices behave.

Therefore, the Federal Reserve and the administration reached a conscious and coordinated decision that the monetary brakes should be released and not reapplied. The Federal Reserve welcomed the opportunity to support a safe rebuilding of the nation's depleted liquidity in the first half of 1967. After a period of severe monetary restraint, a return to a normal national balance sheet in a prosperous environment required above-average growth of money and credit. Even after midyear, a rather accommodating monetary policy was maintained, despite the Federal Reserve's and the administration's assessment that a dangerous new boom was emerging. The right course for monetary policy depended on expectations about fiscal action. Since the tax proposal was explicitly designed as an alternative to tight money, a restrictive monetary policy would have undermined the economic and political case for the tax increase.

The Federal Reserve pursued a monetary policy that was deemed appropriate on the assumption that prompt tax action was forthcoming. This proved to be a losing bet, and perhaps it was a bad bet ex ante. Second-guessers are entitled to their field day on the 1967 decisions of the Federal Reserve. But they ought to observe one rule of fair play—to recognize the interrelationship between the fiscal and monetary decisions of that period.

Fiscal Stalemate

As it turned out, Congress was unwilling to raise taxes in 1967 on the basis of a forecast of acceleration. The main argument against the tax increase was that the case for economic restraint had not been proved: The economy admittedly was not yet going too fast, our price record was better than it had been, and so were financial markets and our international trade surplus. Congress would not act on a forecast; it wanted facts.

The forecast of an acceleration in economic activity was rooted in the facts of the situation. Final sales had advanced rapidly in the first half of 1967, paced by the continued increase of defense expenditures and the rebound in homebuilding. The overall gains in GNP had, however, been very modest because of a record-breaking downswing in inventory accumulation. As of midyear, there was no reason to expect the growth of final sales to slow appreciably and every reason to believe that the inventory adjustment was largely behind us. These two judgments translated into a diagnosis of an accelerating economy.[17]

17. Testimony of Gardner Ackley on August 14, 1967, *President's 1967 Tax Proposals,* Hearings before the House Committee on Ways and Means, 90 Cong. 1 sess. (1967), Pt. 1, pp. 48–61.

In response to congressional demands for facts rather than forecasts, administration spokesmen repeatedly pointed out that "it is impossible . . . to have an intelligent economic and fiscal policy without some kind of a forecast. . . . a forecast is always necessary in evaluating a fiscal program." [18]

It was emphasized that inaction on taxes was action to create a major additional fiscal stimulus. That stimulus could be justified only by accepting the implausible forecast that economic activity was not going to speed up. Congress did not have a choice between acting and not acting, between operating on forecasts or waiting for facts; it could only choose among alternative fiscal programs and among alternative forecasts.

Many independent professional economists backed up the administration's verdict and few dissented, as I noted in Chapter 1. But the Congress was not persuaded. On November 30, in adjourning the Hearings before the House Ways and Means Committee for the 1967 congressional session, Chairman Wilbur Mills summarized: "I have not seen as yet any evidence that we are currently in any demand-pull inflationary situation which requires immediate action. . . ." [19]

The skepticism of the Congress was buttressed by widespread opposition of the general public to higher taxes. It is easy to be sympathetic with the man on the street when he resists the unpleasant medicine of a tax increase. He has good reason to be skeptical that he can enhance his welfare by sacrificing 1 percent of his income in the form of higher income taxes. The dent in his take-home pay associated with higher taxes is obvious and definite; the prospect that he will thereby get insurance against inflation and high interest rates and a better chance for long-run prosperity is highly speculative and uncertain. The argument sounds to him like a familiar con game: Just give me your money and I'll make you rich.

18. *Ibid.*, p. 80.
19. *President's 1967 Surtax Proposal: Continuation of Hearing To Receive Further Administration Proposal Concerning Expenditure Cuts —November 1967,* Hearings before the House Committee on Ways and Means, 90 Cong. 1 sess. (1967), p. 200.

Nor could popular support for the tax bill be marshaled by a patriotic appeal to finance the war. A number of old pro politicians offered marketing advice to administration officials on how to sell the surcharge: Wrap the tax increase in the American flag and forget all the fancy arguments about economic consequences. This formula had worked well enough for the Second World War and Korea, but it could not apply to a limited war which was itself unpopular with many Americans. President Johnson did, in fact, repeatedly use the war argument as well as other arguments.[20] And he knew its limitations; as he said: "I know it is not a popular thing for a President to do . . . to ask anyone for a penny out of a dollar to pay for a war that is not popular either. . . ." [21]

The need for economic restraint became clear to the Congress and the public early in 1968 when the horror stories of the economic forecasts began to come true. Prices accelerated to a 4 percent rate of increase; interest rates rose far above their 1966 peaks; and our world trade surplus again shrank. The economy moved into a feverish boom with a huge advance in GNP of $19 billion in the first quarter of 1968.

Even so, it took major efforts by the American business community and the world financial community to dramatize the urgency of the need for fiscal restraint. With gratifying sophistication and public spirit, our business leaders lined up solidly and vocally behind the tax increase. The advocacy of bankers and homebuilders for higher taxes could be discounted because they were so vulnerable to tight money, but when industrialists traveled to Washington to volunteer—indeed, to demand—to pay higher taxes, our legislators were greatly impressed. The plea was so obviously contrary to the immediate selfish interests of the petitioners that it could be attributed only to a deeply felt sense of the public interest.

The threat of international financial crisis may well have

20. A selection of these presidential statements is found in *The 1968 Economic Report of the President,* Hearings before the Joint Economic Committee, 90 Cong. 2 sess. (1968), Pt. 1, pp. 26–27.

21. *Ibid.,* p. 27.

been the single most decisive factor in getting Congress to move on fiscal restraint. The devaluation of sterling in November 1967 was an event extraneous to U.S. economic conditions. But, by generating serious uncertainties in international financial markets, it made the dollar particularly vulnerable to attack. As a result, internal U.S. conditions were subjected to intensive scrutiny throughout the world. Our legislative stalemate on taxes was read abroad as a threat of failure of the democratic process in the United States and a clear indication that we lacked the will to keep our economic affairs under control. In the spring of 1968, the United States was not a well-managed bank; and its depositors—foreign central bankers—were understandably nervous.

Few Americans comprehend the nature and economic significance of an international financial crisis. But the specter of "the downfall of the dollar" makes a much more frightening picture than the threat of an acceleration of one or two percentage points in prices or interest rates. The pleas and threats, the cajolery and rebukes of central bankers around the world had a major impact on our political process. Suddenly, the words of conservative international bankers became music to the ears of liberal American economists. Without the world bankers, I seriously doubt that we would have enacted the fiscal program that was so urgently needed for our own good.

Breaking the Stalemate

Once the need for restraint in stabilization policy was generally recognized, debate centered on the nature of the restraint. There was a clear social consensus against tight money, and hence nearly universal support for the official verdict expressed by the Council of Economic Advisers:

> After a hard look at the alternatives, it has been and remains the conviction of both the Administration and the Federal Reserve System that the Nation should depend on fiscal policy, not monetary policy, to carry the main burden of the additional restraint on the growth of demand that now appears necessary for 1968.[22]

22. *Annual Report of the CEA, 1968*, pp. 84–85.

Controversy centered on the precise mix of budget cutbacks and tax increases in a program of fiscal restraint. There had been a harbinger of this issue in 1967, when a few members of the Congress—most notably Senator John J. Williams and Representative John W. Byrnes—had expressed their support for a tax increase provided that it was coupled with a sufficient cutback in expenditures. In the spring of 1968, many others in the Congress embraced the spending issue and reversed their earlier opposition to higher taxes.

Even with a general consensus in favor of fiscal restraint, it was not evident whether any coalition on the Hill was large enough to enact any particular package. Some favored a tax increase only if it were linked to an expenditure cutback; others were for higher taxes only if the extra revenues helped to protect expenditure programs; still others argued that a tax reform to improve equity must be coupled with any tax increase.

Secretary Fowler, who brilliantly and tirelessly handled the administration's legislative strategy, convinced the President that an agreement with the budget cutters offered the best hope for enacting a program of fiscal restraint. Hence President Johnson accepted a ceiling on federal expenditures as part of a tie-in sale with the surcharge, even though the principle of the expenditure ceiling was anathema to the administration—much more so than the program cutbacks imposed by the ceiling.

President Johnson naturally recognized the congressional prerogative of rejecting or pruning down, through the traditional appropriations process, any presidential request for funds. His strong resistance and the extreme reluctance of his ultimate concession were focused on the unprecedented technique whereby Congress told the President *how much* to cut his budget without telling him *where* to cut it. As always, Congress reviewed each program in its appropriations process and established, program by program, the desirable level of funding. But simultaneously, for the first time in history, it enacted a ceiling on total spending, telling the President that he must not spend as much as Congress itself had deemed to be socially necessary in its review of appropriations. One would think that the whole ought to equal the sum of the parts even on Capitol Hill.

The Stubborn Boom

The Revenue and Expenditure Control Act of 1968 was signed by President Johnson on June 28. It provided at long last the 10 percent surcharge on corporate and individual incomes that had been requested nearly a year earlier; the surcharge was applied retroactively to April 1 on individual incomes and to January 1 on corporate incomes. The surcharge was coupled with a $6 billion cutback in expenditures for fiscal year 1969, exempting special costs of Vietnam and uncontrollable federal outlays. In combination, these measures represented a very marked shift in the federal budget toward restraint.

It was hoped and expected that this legislative victory would usher in a period of gradual disinflation. The target path of economic activity called for growth of output at a rate substantially less than the potential growth of the economy for about a year. Such a slow pace necessarily entailed a regrettable upcreep in unemployment. A real growth rate of about 2 percent between mid-1968 and mid-1969 was expected to push the unemployment rate up slightly above 4 percent from its 3½ percent level of the time. The reduced pressure on resources and the increased discipline of competition would then curb inflation. Price and wage increases obviously had substantial momentum and could not be halted in their tracks, but it was a reasonable judgment—supported by the experience of 1967—that an economic environment of slow advance would produce a gradual and progressive deceleration of the price-wage spiral.

Actual developments did not follow the flight plan. The slowdown was not nearly so pronounced as had been anticipated. Still, economic activity did change pace. If GNP had advanced as rapidly in the five quarters after the enactment of the fiscal program as it had in the preceding two quarters, it would have been $965 billion rather than the $942 billion actually reached in the third quarter of 1969. The moderation in the growth rate of real output was more marked—from 6½ percent in the first half of 1968 to 3½ percent in the second half and 2½ percent in the first half of 1969.

Nevertheless, the boom proved remarkably stubborn, and the experience was a sobering one for many economic diagnosticians, forecasters, and policy planners. If I seem defensive in reviewing the results, it is only because I am.

The height of the patient's fever was misdiagnosed in the spring of 1968, and consequently the dose of medicine administered to bring it down was inadequate. We did not realize how much boom fever had developed while the fiscal program was being debated. In particular, we misread some evidence provided by certain statistical indicators as signals of moderation in private demand. Some of these signals seemed to be coming from the consumer sector. Consumption outlays in the spring were considerably lower than was to be expected on the basis of their past relationship to incomes. Many forecasters projected a continuation of this development. But it proved transitory when the consumer showed new life in the summer of 1968. The gain in the annual rate of consumer expenditures jumped from $9.7 billion in the second quarter to $14.6 billion in the third. That $5 billion acceleration, associated with a constant rate of advance of before-tax household incomes, remains a puzzle even if one assumes that consumer spending was totally immune to the surcharge in its initial quarter of operation.

On my own work sheets as of mid-1968, the surcharge, which began to affect pay checks through withholding on July 15, was expected to reduce the increment of consumption in the third quarter by $2 billion. We do not know and cannot tell whether or not the surcharge had such an effect, compared with the increase that would have otherwise occurred. We do know that the main reason consumption exceeded the forecasts was not that we were wrong about the impact of the surcharge but that we were wrong about the emerging strength of consumer demand, quite apart from the surcharge. The evidence indicates that, if no surcharge had been enacted, a marked strengthening in consumer demand would have been experienced. This is important, not only because I prefer to be hanged for the crime I committed, but because it suggests that the main thing wrong with the medicine of fiscal restraint was the delayed and inadequate dosage.

Another important misleading signal came from homebuilding. Housing starts dropped off sharply in May and June, and that decline seemed genuine enough in light of developments in mortgage interest rates. Yet despite high and rising mortgage interest rates and despite wide differentials between yields on securities and those on thrift deposits such as led to a major outflow of funds from thrift institutions in 1966, homebuilding surged ahead later in the year. Some of the differences between 1966 and 1968 are evident: Deposits in thrift institutions were less responsive to yield differentials in 1968 because much of the interest-sensitive "hot money" withdrawn in 1966 had not returned; homebuilding got more support in 1968 from the Federal National Mortgage Association, the Federal Home Loan Bank Board, and other federal aids; the basic demand for new homes was dramatically stronger in 1968; and lenders were attracted by "equity kickers," a major financial innovation that turned mortgages on apartments into the equivalent of convertible bonds. All of these factors still leave a partial mystery about where the funds came from to finance residential construction late in 1968 and early in 1969. And the gloomy signals in the spring of 1968 remain unexplained. Were they merely statistical flukes, or was there a brief period of uncertainty in financing that was ended by the enactment of the fiscal program?

Because the outlook for homebuilding seemed bleak and that for the economy as a whole appeared moderate, the Federal Reserve celebrated the enactment of the fiscal program with some easing, supporting and following bullish developments in financial markets. This turned out to be the wrong policy because it was the right policy for what turned out to be the wrong forecast. And, in believing that erroneous forecast, the Federal Reserve had lots of company—at the Council and among other government forecasters and business economists. The monetary decisions made in the summer and fall of 1968 could not conceivably have had a significant influence on economic activity during 1968, but they did contribute to continued overexuberance in 1969.

After the surprises in housing and consumption were revealed, plant and equipment spending produced the biggest surprise of all. Although sales and profits had been forging strongly ahead, business capital outlays had been rather sluggish during most of 1968, rising only 4 percent for the year as a whole. But at year-end, there was a remarkable display of new strength in investment demand, followed by a further scaling up of capital budgets early in 1969.

It is easy to speculate about, and hard to find any fully convincing explanation for, the performance of business fixed investment. Inflationary expectations are sometimes identified as the culprit, inducing businessmen to speed up their procurement of buildings and machines before prices rose further. No doubt such considerations must have been important in some cases, particularly in construction projects where costs were moving up rapidly. But the lofty levels of market interest rates —which also reflected price expectations—should have offset much of the incentive to beat rising prices to the punch. Moreover, the behavior of inventories suggests that inflationary expectations could not generally have dominated business decision making. It is surely easier to hedge against or speculate on price rises by holding added inventories of materials than by rescheduling capital projects; yet inventory demand was geared conservatively to needs throughout the period. Perhaps the most relevant expectations were those of rapidly rising labor costs and continuing tightness of labor markets; these may have encouraged labor-saving capital projects.

Perhaps expectations of long-term prosperity—rather than expectations of inflation—enhanced the appeal of investment.

After four years in which expansion and investment had generally been profitable, businessmen may have been prepared to count on the long-run buoyancy of demand even when some current indicators pointed the other way. This may be a reverse image of the 1962 experience when investment demand was weak even though final demand had strengthened; at that time, after five years of economic slack, the capital budgeteers refused to fire until they saw the green of the consumer's dollar. Perhaps the nagging uncertainties about government policy earlier in 1968 had delayed some investment decisions and masked the underlying strength of business capital spending. In that case, we would have to learn the paradoxical lesson that uncertainty about the nature of a policy of restraint may temporarily have a restraining effect even greater than that of the actual restraining measures.

The puzzles of 1968–69 raise important questions about the proper formula for halting a boom without causing a recession. Is it generally true that, when the atmosphere is fundamentally bullish, a large dose of restrictive medicine is necessary to get results? Perhaps, in a boom situation, increased taxes are likely to curtail spending less, and correspondingly reduce saving more, than normally. Perhaps, in a boom, the impact of tighter money may be generally blunted by inelastic demands for funds and a speeding up of the velocity of circulation. If the public has intense desires for goods and services, it may be willing to dip into savings, to incur debt, and to economize on cash balances and liquidity, thus offsetting partially the restrictive impact of fiscal-monetary measures. If this hypothesis has any validity, it would underline the dangers of allowing a boom to get a firm foothold.

The temporary character of the income tax surcharge raised another question: Would it have had a much greater restraining impact if it had been enacted for a very long period? I believe there is compelling evidence that consumers gear their living standards in part to expectations of long-run income. Hence permanent changes in income generate larger responses in their spending than changes they view as temporary.

Viewing the surcharge in advance, I felt that some discount
on its restraining effect should be taken for its temporary character. There was no certainty about the right size of the discount, but 20 or 25 percent seemed to be in the ballpark. Such
a figure was consistent with empirical studies of the difference
in impact between long- and short-run changes in income.
Furthermore, the estimate had to reflect the widespread skepticism, bolstered in part by the history of Korean war taxation, as to whether the surcharge would in fact remain temporary. Finally, the surcharge was just one of a dozen major
economic features that consumers might pass off as temporary
—income from opportunities to work overtime; unusually large
wage increases; jobs which depended on the defense emergency;
the squeeze of inflation on some real incomes. It did not, and
still does not, seem plausible that consumers would factor the
surcharge out as the one temporary element in their household
income statement. If the personal saving rate moves up again
for an extended period after the surcharge expires, that will
point to a higher estimate of the appropriate discount. But it
would be premature to make that judgment now.

The difficulties of explaining the movements of private demand and the responses to public policy during 1968–69 remind us of how much economists have to learn. They also
remind us that changes in attitudes in the private economy can
at times swamp decisions of public policy. They argue for
humility in our discussions of the economic outlook and for
flexibility in the making of policy. But they offer no excuse
for inaction. The steps taken to moderate the boom worked
in the right direction and would have been more effective if
they had been taken sooner.

The surge in private demand forced policy makers to take
some extra notches in the fiscal-monetary belt during 1969.
These adjustments were a flexible and appropriate response to
new developments. The Nixon administration demonstrated a
commitment to continued prosperity and to a gradual attack
on inflation. The basic objectives and the means of attaining
them reaffirm those under the Johnson administration. The
general strategy of stabilization policy has become bipartisan.

Summary

The economy and economic policy have followed a complicated and difficult course in the latter half of the sixties. It is very easy and very tempting to suppress all this in a simple caricature that is all bright or all gloomy. If you want to paint a rosy picture, emphasize the following: Corrected for inflation, the real income of the average American—disposable personal income per capita in constant prices—rose 15 percent from the second quarter of 1965 to the third quarter of 1969. At least 8 million people escaped from poverty in that period. At no time has the real output of the economy deviated from the target of potential by more than 2 percent; no other four-year period in our history can make such a claim. Even our price record has not been bad by the standard of previous periods of hostilities; and it was achieved without the damaging restrictions of price and wage controls. Despite political constraints and despite the uncertainties and disruptions of the defense buildup, an alert and ingenious Federal Reserve and a determined executive branch have kept the economy progressing with unparalleled prosperity.

It might be hard to recognize the same economy in the following gloomy story: Our recent price performance has been the worst in eighteen years. Many interest rates are at their highest levels in a century. Because of inflation, millions of Americans experienced declines in their real net worth. Fiscal and monetary policy stimulated the economy too long and too hard in 1965. Monetary policy was then shifted abruptly toward restraint in 1966, sending our homebuilding industry into a depression and nearly panicking our financial markets. The investment tax credit was taken off in the fall of 1966— a fiscal action that was too little and too late to do much good. The credit was then hurriedly put back in place early in 1967. While the big tax debate was being conducted, the Federal Reserve did not restrain an emerging boom. Then when the fiscal package was enacted, an erroneous assessment held that no further monetary restraint was needed. A retreat from that position was necessary at the end of 1968 and further fallbacks were required during 1969.

Neither of these caricatures is very illuminating. Obviously, things could have been better and they could have been worse. The bright spots in the record stem largely from flexibility and resiliency in both the private economy and public policy. Private demand has not been on a tight rope. It has kept its balance, on the whole, despite the mistakes of public policy. Similarly, the makers of economic policy showed flexibility: a willingness to make adjustments, to concede errors, to rechart the course, and to use all available political elbow room to move toward the target. On both the public and the private sides, our economy demonstrated that it is not brittle.

The flaws of the performance can be attributed to three types of factors: (1) the uncertainties and disruptions of defense spending; (2) political resistance to the unpleasant medicine of economic restraint; and (3) the limitations and errors of technical economic analysis.

These factors have interacted to an important degree. Political resistance to economic restraint was reinforced by the unpopularity of the war. Legislators undoubtedly find it easier to disregard recommendations for unpleasant actions because they know that the economist's advice is highly fallible. There is room for progress on all three fronts. As I pointed out above, however, some costs to economic stability are inevitable in a period of unstable defense spending. Moreover, the advances in technical economic analysis are likely to proceed slowly and gradually. Improvements in political attitudes seem the most promising route to progress. There is a continuing need for more public understanding and public acceptance of the economics of restraint.

A great deal of the effort of the political economist must continue to be concentrated on the elementary pedagogy of stabilization policy. During the surcharge battle, I found it as important to produce homilies about small boys taking medicine and fat ladies munching candy as to work on forecasts and technical analyses.[23] The basic lessons must be taught—and learned—if we are to close the regrettably large gap between our potential and actual performance in economic policy.

23. ". . . Some recent public utterances against the tax increase remind me strongly of my 7-year-old son's arguments against taking medicine. All in one breath, he can reel off a multitude of objections: he is perfectly well; he is so sick that nothing can possibly help him; it may, indeed, cure his sore throat but would surely give him an even more painful stomach ache; he will take it later in the day if his throat doesn't get better; he would have taken the medicine without a fuss if his mother had given it to him the day before; it isn't fair unless his brothers take it too. A small boy finds it hard to accept the need to do something unpleasant in order to avoid even worse consequences. But maturity helps; my two older sons take their medicine without much fuss." Arthur M. Okun, "Prospects for the Economy" (remarks at the Second Annual Economic Forecasting Conference of the National Account Marketing Association, New York City, Sept. 22, 1967; processed).

"We have already seen the costs of delay build up gradually to a huge sum. This is not a case where the next straw is likely to break the camel's back. A better analogy may be a fat lady munching candy. Nobody can promise her a lovely figure overnight if she stops nibbling. Nobody can legitimately warn her that one more piece would do incalculable damage. And forgoing the candy means sacrificing a lot of fun in the short run. But the more she overindulges, the more serious the risks become. The time to stop our economic overindulgence is now" (remarks at the National Press Club, Washington, April 18, 1968; processed).

chapter four

The Agenda for Stabilization Policy

Can the United States have high-employment prosperity without inflation? For some time, the American people have been asked to tune in tomorrow and find out; but the last episode of the serial has not yet been produced. In no period during the past forty years has the American economy been free of excessive unemployment *and* inflationary tendencies simultaneously. Nor has any other industrial nation found the happy combination. Hitting the dual target of high utilization and essential price stability remains the most serious unsolved problem of stabilization policy throughout the Western world.

Prosperity without Inflation

In principle, the problem of achieving high employment without inflation has no perfect solution. Society will always be faced with an opportunity to get more output and more employment—at least in the short run—by heating up the economy. But the hotter the state of demand, the greater the pressures of inflation.

On the other hand, we can ensure price stability by operating a slack economy. If markets are sufficiently weak, no businessman will dare raise his prices for fear of losing his markets, and no workers—organized or unorganized—will demand significant wage increases for fear of losing their jobs. However, this is the decapitation cure for the headache of inflation. Stabilization policy must take account of both high employment and price stability, and it must find the middle of the road.

From the summer of 1965 to the autumn of 1966 and, again, for a long time after the summer of 1967, the economy was off the middle of the road. We experienced a seller's market for both goods and labor, and hence unacceptable rates of increase in both prices and wages. A return to the middle of the road simply could not be accomplished without a retreat from the 3.3 percent unemployment rate that prevailed early in 1969. And so economists were obliged to tell the nation an unhappy fact of life: If the American public wanted a better price performance, it had to accept some increase in unemployment.

In a gradual restoration of reasonable price stability, the rise in unemployment can be fairly small and a recession certainly need not be part of the prescription. To be sure, a gradual cure of inflation, accomplished without recession, takes much longer than radical surgery. The 1957–58 experience suggests that the latter course could give us a good price performance within a year or so, while the gradual strategy may take several years to accomplish fully its aim. But a number of decisive arguments favor the slow cure.

First and foremost, gradual disinflation minimizes the sacrifice of jobs, output, and real incomes required to achieve the objective. In our last two recessions, the unemployment rate reached 7 percent. A repetition of that experience could cost the nation nearly $100 billion of output and real incomes; over $30 billion of before-tax profits; an extra 3 million persons below the line of poverty income; and the loss of about 5 million man-years of labor. Can anyone doubt that these costs would exceed those of the entire recent four-year period of inflation?

Second, whatever the target rate of unemployment we adopt for the long run, it is likely to be accompanied by a better price performance if approached by the gradual route than by a quick retreat into recession followed by a new spurt. Suppose the unemployment rate in 1972–74 is to be 4 (or 3¾ or 4¼) percent. There are two ways of getting there: One allows unemployment to creep up gradually; the other has 7 percent unemployment in the short run followed, of necessity, by a rapid advance in economic activity thereafter. Because a period of especially rapid economic advance impairs price performance, prices in 1974 will be more stable along the gradualist route than in the retreat-and-spurt strategy.

Finally, the crying need for reliable information about the basic price-wage performance of our economy in prosperity is an important argument in favor of a gradual cure of inflation. In the process of moving gradually toward price stability, we will learn a lot about what our economy can really do in prosperity. The recession strategy would postpone the essential test that we must ultimately face of simultaneously attaining high employment and an acceptable price performance. Once we began a renewed move toward full employment after the retreat, we would again face the dilemma of when and where to stop with no more information than we have now.

Over the longer run, the big question will be what the middle of the road looks like. On an optimistic-realistic view, the best hope is that a 4 percent rate of unemployment and a 2 percent annual rate of price increase will prove compatible and that such a combination will be regarded as a satisfactory compromise by the American public. This was the hope before the Vietnam spurt in mid-1965, and nothing that has happened since then demonstrates that it is unattainable. It is true, of course, that the achievement of 4 percent unemployment was associated with an acceleration of prices to a much higher rate. But the economy's price performance in 1966 (and again in 1968) was influenced by the exceptionally rapid advance of economic activity as well as by the high levels of utilization.

Spurts in demand create more upward pressures on prices and labor costs than would occur from reaching the same level of utilization along a smoother path. Supply is more elastic in the long run than in the short run. It takes time to adjust the output of agricultural and mining raw materials; when demand rises sharply, most of the impact is reflected in higher prices rather than increased production. Business firms can add employees in bottleneck areas, but there is a limit to the rate at which they can hire and train new people or upgrade their existing workers.

These spurts prevented us from determining just how well our economy could, with its existing institutions, meet our desires for both high employment and essential price stability. Whether the 4–2 combination is economically feasible and politically acceptable remains to be seen. And we will see if we back up on our utilization rate gradually.

The Institutional Framework

What we see will also depend on how much we improve our institutional framework. There is nothing immutable about the intensity of competition or the mobility of resources in our economy. These factors are influenced by a host of decisions in the private economy and by a multitude of government policies. Regulatory actions, international trade policies, antitrust laws and their implementation, government research and development programs, procurement techniques, and farm price supports are just some of the federal decisions that affect the price-cost structure. Indeed, the employment-inflation tradeoff is influenced by every federal economic policy except fiscal and monetary policies. The budgetary and credit tools can help by avoiding spurts in activity. But improving the terms of the tradeoff is essentially beyond their power and scope.

For this reason, our efforts to achieve noninflationary prosperity should not rest entirely on monetary and fiscal policy. By reviewing and improving its impact on the structure of prices and costs, the government can enhance our ability to attain a satisfactory compromise between maximum employment and essential price stability. Moreover, the government can tailor its manpower programs and its support of particular industries —like construction and health care—to break bottlenecks and improve the institutional structure in which prices and wages are set. President Johnson established the Cabinet Committee on Price Stability in 1968 to coordinate the attack on these structural problems.[1] Parts of this work are continuing under

1. See *Economic Report of the President together with the Annual Report of the Council of Economic Advisers, February 1968*, pp. 19–20, and . . . *January 1969*, pp. 98–122; and *Studies by the Staff of the Cabinet Committee on Price Stability* (1969).

the Nixon administration. There is much unfinished business in this area and it deserves high priority.

Finally, a comprehensive program to achieve noninflationary prosperity should include a major effort to enlist the voluntary cooperation of large firms and unions with substantial market power. Prices and wages in the American economy reflect both market competition and market power. In many important areas, management and labor have a good deal of discretion over prices and wages. How they exercise that discretion is influenced by the attitudes of the federal government. When, at the start of the Nixon administration, the President expressed his strong opposition to the use of the jawbone, his words were interpreted as a declaration of open season for price and wage increases. And that judgment was reflected in the prices of many concentrated industries. The price record of gasoline, automobiles, steel, copper, and other metals was far worse during 1969 than 1968. No one of these areas offers decisive evidence, but together they compel the conclusion that the change in the rules of the game led to a speed-up of administered prices.

Once the government began to carry out properly its job of fiscal-monetary restraint, it moved into an excellent position to ask for help from private decision makers. To capitalize on that opportunity, we need a new program of voluntary restraint. I believe the essential ingredients for such a system can be identified in light of the experiences—and the mistakes—of the Kennedy and Johnson administrations.

First, in seeking cooperation from private decision makers, the government must carefully ensure that its actions promote a noninflationary environment. Discipline in fiscal and monetary policy is the first requirement. And the structural policies that influence prices and costs must also be in harmony. To take a notable example, the government cannot reasonably ask private workers to restrain their wage demands if the pay scales of public employees are shooting ahead.

Second, the appeal for restraint must be based on some set of ground rules that spell out what private decision makers are being asked to do. "Drive carefully" is not an effective substitute for a posted speed limit. Speed limits on wages and prices will inevitably share some of the imperfections of those on the highways. They will contain an element of arbitrariness, just as a fifty-mile speed limit is arbitrary in the sense that it is not demonstrably superior to forty-nine or fifty-one. Just as a passing lane is needed on the highways, so a "passing lane" must be provided for wages and prices, allowing relative shifts over time in response to the signals of the market. Just as some speeders will escape the eyes of the traffic patrol, so some violators of the price and wage standards will not be identified. Despite their imperfections, speed limits on the highways serve the nation well and so can those on prices and wages.

Third, the standards should be developed only after the fullest consultation with business and labor. Private groups should have every opportunity to express their views and to identify problems that might not otherwise be recognized. Persuasion can be most effective when it is coupled with representation.

Fourth, the one sanction essential and appropriate in a voluntary restraint program is the force of public opinion. Flagrant violations of the standards must be exposed to public scrutiny. But, except for the glare of the spotlight, violators should have impunity. The one issue that may pose difficult questions is the appropriate use of procurement, stockpiles, and tax and foreign trade policies to serve the cause of price stability.

Fifth, because many price and wage decisions are complex, some responsible and competent umpire must call foul balls. But to minimize shouting matches, the umpire should be at least an arm's length away from the President. And that means farther away than his Council of Economic Advisers. I see great merit in Congressman Henry Reuss's proposal that the umpire should be a small special advisory board on price and wage standards. Its members should be experienced in the decision process of the collective bargaining table and the top management meeting, but should not be active partisans at the time of their appointment. Some of our labor mediators and arbitrators and some of our business school deans could carry out this assignment with distinction. The group should be appointed by the President and should consult with executive agencies as well as private and congressional groups. It should be explicitly authorized to issue public statements and reports without clearing them through the administration.

I cannot be confident that such a system would function effectively. But I am confident that an experiment along these lines is worth the effort. By not trying hard enough currently, we are handicapping our efforts to reconcile prosperity and price stability. And we cannot afford even a small handicap in this vital and difficult contest.

Welfare Aspects of the Tradeoff

The economics profession and the nation need better analytical criteria by which to balance the costs of a little more up-creep in prices with those of a little more unemployment. The enormous social costs associated with galloping inflation are easy to document in the experience of some other nations; they can lead to the breakdown of the financial system and the network of exchange and specialization. But these inefficiencies do not seem to emerge continuously as prices accelerate, and it is not clear that they apply at all to situations of moderate inflation (say, 5 percent a year). Plainly, even moderate inflation can severely damage the balance-of-payments position of a nation which is inflating faster than its trading partners. But the gut political issues about inflation involve the costs on the home front, and these are elusive. Because economists do not have good solid answers, they are tempted either to get moralistic about price stability, or else, on the other extreme, to dismiss the problem of inflation as an optical illusion. I don't have good answers, but I promise neither to moralize nor to dismiss the problem.

The costs of a sacrifice of output and employment are fairly obvious—it is not hard to identify the costs to the disadvantaged workers who are likely to be first fired, to the corporations that continue to bear heavy burdens of fixed costs when production tapers off, and to state and local governments that lose revenues needed to finance public expenditures. The costs to the poor are most visible and most serious socially. Yet the income lost by those who become unemployed—many of whom are not poor—is less than half of the total loss of income associated with a slack economy. We all share the waste. We could and should share the loss more equitably through better unemployment compensation and improved income supports for the jobless poor. But the deadweight loss of output and national income is the inescapable cost of a slack economy.

The costs of inflation are harder to measure and to translate into comparable terms. Many generalizations are just plain wrong. It is not generally true that inflation hurts workers as a group, or the poor as a group.[2] The retired aged are the only specific demographic group of Americans that can be confidently identified as victims of an inflationary economy. An arithmetic identity ensures that, for every extra dollar that a buyer must pay as a result of price increases, an extra dollar's worth of income is generated for some seller. That identity does not render inflation costless, but it does make it obvious why the costs cannot be simply defined. Indeed, it is precisely because higher prices raise money incomes in a haphazard, apparently arbitrary way, that there is so much anguish about inflation. The resulting redistribution of income does not even seem to create desirable incentives to shift production or to move resources. Such a reshuffling of real incomes is, in the view of most Americans, unjust.

Moreover, the effects of inflation in raising money incomes may be less visible than the higher prices. Everybody knows that higher prices in our supermarkets and department stores are the result of inflation. When money incomes go up, however, the cause is not so obvious. When the man of the house brings home an 8 percent wage increase, he and his wife are confident that he earned and deserved that raise. If prices subsequently go up by 4 percent, the family is not happy with the

2. See Robinson G. Hollister and John L. Palmer, *The Impact of Inflation on the Poor* (Institute for Research on Poverty, University of Wisconsin, 1969).

4 percent gain in real income; rather, it feels cheated that the wage gain was cut in half by inflation. In point of fact, of course, the husband's 8 percent wage increase may have occurred only because of inflation. Nonetheless, nearly everybody feels that inflation leaves him with the short end of the stick. It is thus divisive and disruptive; and these social consequences cannot be ignored.

The effects of inflation on people's balance sheets seem particularly serious. When prices are rising rapidly, their exact course is bound to be unpredictable. In such a situation, the saver is deprived of the opportunity to provide effectively for the proverbial rainy day, for no asset offers a dependable command over consumer goods in the future. In the case of liquid assets, purchasing power declines as consumer prices rise. Real estate and corporate equities, though they may fare well over the long run, are subject to wide swings and great uncertainties. Some sophisticated savers may manage to reap gains on inflation, while other savers are hurt. Inflation thereby creates an unhappy division of savers into "sharpies" and "suckers," if I may borrow some nontechnical terminology.

Some recent economic research stresses the danger that inflation may feed on itself and accelerate through time.[3] Under some assumptions about the workings of markets, the extra employment and output associated with excess total demand would either vanish ultimately or else be accompanied by accelerating prices. Assuming that society will not accept ever faster rates of price increase, it cannot maintain the bonus of output and jobs permanently in the world of this model. Thus, in the long run, the tradeoff disappears. Given the institutional structure, society cannot opt for a maintained unemployment rate below some "natural" minimum.

This model surely has some relevance to the real world.

3. See Milton Friedman, "The Role of Monetary Policy," *American Economic Review,* Vol. 58 (March 1968), pp. 1–17; Edmund S. Phelps, "The New Microeconomics in Inflation and Employment Theory," in American Economic Association, *Papers and Proceedings of the Eighty-first Annual Meeting, 1968 (American Economic Review,* Vol. 59, May 1969), pp. 147–60.

Many of the beneficial side effects of inflation seem to depend on surprising, cheating, and frustrating people. Once the "suckers" learn their lesson, a tendency must emerge toward accelerating prices or retreating rates of utilization. Hence proposals designed to help us live with inflation by introducing cost-of-living escalators on bonds and wages might well either speed up inflation or jeopardize the bonus of output and employment. A comprehensive effort to provide insulation against inflation could prevent the cooking as well as the burning.

On the other hand, even if all the vexing tradeoff problems are resolved in the long run, we could not escape our current task of searching for a compromise. The long run is apparently a matter of decades rather than years, to judge from the experience of many nations which have experienced substantial inflation for a long time without succumbing either to pronounced acceleration of prices or a rising trend of unemployment.

The policy maker must face up to the near-term tradeoff and he must be guided by his perception of public attitudes. It is clear that 4 and 5 percent rates of price increase are intolerable to the American public—whether or not they are likely to speed up to 8 and 10 percent.

The Flexibility-Stability Dilemma

Another major unresolved issue in stabilization policy concerns the nature and frequency of changes in policy actions. Several years ago, it was regarded as a truism that economic policy should be flexible. Today we hear the call for greater stability in policy, obviously at the sacrifice of some flexibility. The change in attitudes is readily understood and the latest fashion conveys a message which is well worth hearing. But, as sometimes stated, proposals for inactive policy misread utterly the lessons of the sixties and pose a serious threat to the future stability of American economic performance.

The desire for less motion in stabilization policy reflects some of the experience discussed in Chapter 3. Because of the move-

ments of defense spending and the paralysis of tax rates, economic policy makers had to resort to some inelegant, second-
best techniques of stabilization during recent years—heavy and
shifting reliance on monetary policy, the quick suspension and
restoration of the investment credit, a series of turnabouts in the
posture on nondefense expenditures, excessive dependence on
the jawbone. Notable shortcomings in our forecasting performance have been mixed with some successes. By comparison
with the great expectations some observers had in 1965, there
have been considerable disappointments and a resulting flagging
of enthusiasm for flexible fiscal-monetary policy.

Our businessmen seem particularly concerned about swings
in policy. Because of the shifting fiscal and monetary tides,
businessmen have had to pay more attention to Washington's
actions in recent years than at any time since the Korean war.
The decisions of government on defense spending, taxes, and
credit policy have loomed large in the perspective of the business decision maker. They have been important sources of uncertainty and of disruption to business planning. The businessman has good reason to wish that the economic policy planner
would retreat into a corner, lead a quieter and more contem-
plative life, and take his shadow off the business scene.

In the professional literature, the activist strategy is sometimes lampooned under the heading of "fine tuning." [4] When
Walter Heller coined that phrase—which he now assigns to "the
gallery of gaffes in economic-policy semantics" [5]—he did not
intend to characterize a philosophy of economic policy. The
pretentious ring of that phrase worried me, and I explicitly
rejected it in my first speech as Chairman of the Council of
Economic Advisers:

4. See, for example, Charles B. Reeder, "Business Economists and
National Economic Policy," *Business Economics,* Vol. 3 (Fall 1967),
pp. 7–10; Beryl W. Sprinkel, "The 'New Economics'—Limitations and
Alternatives" (speech presented at the Annual Meeting of the Illinois
Chamber of Commerce, Oct. 27, 1967; processed); George Terborgh,
The New Economics (Washington: Machinery and Allied Products In-
stitute and Council for Technological Advancement, 1968, pp. 166–72.
5. Milton Friedman and Walter W. Heller, *Monetary vs. Fiscal Policy*
(W. W. Norton, 1969), p. 34.

Private demand has a reliable tendency to fluctuate. . . .

In principle, such a fluctuation could be offset by . . . fiscal and monetary policies if the course of demand could be perfectly foreseen. But it can't, and nobody is more aware of that fact of life than the Council of Economic Advisers. We have never claimed or attempted to engage in the practice known as "fine-tuning." [6]

Quite apart from semantics, the switches in policy in recent years have not reflected an effort by economists to keep the economy on some precise, narrow course. We were smart enough to know that we weren't that smart! Rather, the fiscal and monetary measures that were within the economists' reach were used in an effort to offset the major destabilizing impact of increased defense spending.

Here, indeed, is the kernel of truth in the new attitude. If policy-planning economists can prevent the government's own fiscal actions from destabilizing the economy, they will have won the larger share of the battle. Surely, since the Second World War, the economy has jumped the track of stable growth more often and more severely as a result of government actions than autonomous shifts in private demand. The 1950–51 Korean inflation, the 1953–54 post-Korean recession, the 1960 recession, and the Vietnam inflation were fluctuations associated with inappropriate swings in the federal budget.

In every one of these instances, it can be said that the planners of stabilization policy did not do their job effectively. But the defects lay in errors of omission rather than in errors of commission. In each case, some strong force was pushing the budgetary impact in one direction; and the budget was allowed to swing in that direction rather than being neutralized by timely and adequate fiscal action. The actions that were taken for stabilization purposes generally worked in the right direction. One can compile a long list of discretionary policy actions during the postwar era that helped to stabilize the economy— the tight fiscal policy of the late forties, the accord of fiscal-monetary policy in 1951, the tax increases of 1950–51, the de-

6. Arthur M. Okun, "Issues in Preserving Prosperity" (speech delivered to the Economic Club of New York, New York City, March 6, 1968; processed).

cision to allow taxes to be reduced in 1954, the antirecession fiscal and monetary program of 1958, the Kennedy recovery program in 1961, the series of tax cuts and the supportive monetary policy in 1962–65, and the variety of restraining actions taken during the Vietnam period.

On the other side of the ledger, we find only a few stabilization actions which boomeranged. The last few notches of monetary tightening in 1957, the excessive credit restraint of 1959, the excise tax cut just preceding the Vietnam escalation in 1965, and the monetary relaxation in the summer of 1968 are four episodes which may qualify for such a list. Another interesting list might be made of cases where discretionary policy steps widely endorsed by economists were not taken for political reasons: A tax cut in 1958, some fiscal stimulus in 1960, and a tax increase in 1966 would all have been beneficial. The whole record clearly suggests that when stabilization policy erred, it was primarily by acting too little and too late—not too much or too soon.

A world of difference lies between an inactive policy and a policy seeking a stable impact. In 1959–60, for example, the quiet life for the policy planner meant a highly unstable course for the impact of the federal budget. During that brief interval, the full employment surplus jumped from near zero to some $15 billion. This massive shift in fiscal impact did not reflect new programs or new tax actions. Nobody surprised private decision makers or changed the rules of the game. The big swing came from drift; as our growing economy generated much higher —or at least potentially much higher—federal revenues, no offsetting expenditure or tax actions were taken to use that growth dividend. Thus, because policy planners led a quiet life, the budget swung mightily in the direction of restraint.

In the 1965–69 period, any successful effort to neutralize the impact of rising defense outlays would have called for a great deal of activism—more than we experienced. In the face of successive new defense decisions, two or three tax increases and probably several shifts in monetary policy would have been required. Again the troubles lay in errors of omission. Paul Mc-

Cracken turned in a similar verdict in April 1968, when he noted how "automatic" or "passive" policy had been in "letting the budget drift into the present state of massive disequilibrium...."[7]

Proposals for inactive fiscal policy must be carefully distinguished from proposals for stabilizing the federal budget impact.[8] Whatever its merits on other grounds, the proposal that overall fiscal stimulus (or restraint) be stabilized—for example, with a fixed full employment surplus in the budget—does not offer the quiet life to the policy planner or insurance against surprises to the businessman. Quite the contrary. Taken literally, the rule would require some new offsetting measure every time estimates of defense spending are changed, every time Congress alters the President's expenditure program significantly, and every time the estimates of federal revenues at high employment have to be revised in light of new information. The makers of fiscal policy would be as busy as the proverbial one-armed paperhanger if they had to hold the full employment surplus unchanged as the world changes. So long as any part of the fiscal program is outside the control of economic policy planners, it is impossible to have both a stable impact and a quiet life.

Of course, no advocate of a stabilized budget impact really proposes to chase every development anywhere in the federal budget. Liberally interpreted as a benchmark or guideline rather than a hard and fast rule, the recommendation for a fixed fiscal impact could help to spotlight the unintended shift and drift in the federal budget. But the proposal rests on two fundamental tenets which I cannot accept. First, it implies that we can be wiser in determining the right size of the full employment sur-

7. Paul W. McCracken, "Federal Expenditure Policy," in American Bankers Association, *Proceedings of a Symposium on the Federal Budget in a Dynamic Economy* (ABA, 1968), p. 114.

8. For a discussion of proposals for a stable fiscal impact, see Committee for Economic Development, *Taxes and the Budget: A Program for Prosperity in a Free Economy* (CED, 1947); Walter W. Heller, "CED's Stabilizing Budget Policy after Ten Years," *American Economic Review,* Vol. 47 (September 1957), pp. 634–51. In its recent statements, CED has articulately stressed the need for flexibility in fiscal policy.

plus for a substantial period of time than in making judgments year by year about whether it should be increased or decreased somewhat. The logic of this view escapes me. It seems far more risky and pretentious to freeze a once-and-for-all estimate of the proper setting of the dial than to try to learn from experience and to adjust the (gross—not fine) tuning over time.

Second, the focus on stabilizing fiscal impact rather than economic performance has strange corollaries. It surely implies a willingness to take offsetting policy action when Congress adds a large amount to federal expenditure programs but not when an even larger surprise is registered in the strength of private spending for plant and equipment.

Is there any case for such an asymmetrical recipe? I find it hard to understand. Whether designed to compensate for movements elsewhere in the public sector or a shift in private demand, stabilization decisions need to take full account of the costs of manipulating the dials of tax rates, federal expenditure programs, or financial conditions. The costs include the loss in efficiency of expenditure programs incurred by stop-go patterns, and the costs to private decision makers of surprises and uncertainties about tax rates and interest rates.

The most compelling arguments against large or frequent turns of the dials stem from the imperfect accuracy of forecasting, the limited distance of the predictive horizon, and the significant time lag in the implementation and economic impact of policy actions. In a world of total ignorance, policy action would be just as likely to push the economy in the wrong direction as in the right direction. And the economy could be pushed off the middle of the road when it would otherwise be there. Thus the best possible strategy for stabilization policy in such a world is to do nothing, regardless of any new developments in either the public or private sector.[9]

On the other extreme, in a world of omniscience and perfect

9. William Brainard, "Uncertainty and the Effectiveness of Policy," in American Economic Association, *Papers and Proceedings of the Seventy-ninth Annual Meeting, 1966 (American Economic Review,* Vol. 57, May 1967), pp. 411–25.

foresight, economic policy actions could simply follow a flight plan formulated far in advance. We could send the navigator on vacation, never use our judgment in appraising new developments, and never surprise anyone. The real world, however, lies somewhere between these extremes. We have enough wisdom to take some prudent actions. But we do not have enough wisdom to fix our course forevermore; we must keep recharting it in light of our errors.

Monetary Rules

The issues of flexibility and stability apply to monetary as well as fiscal policy. The lively professional controversy over the proper criteria for guiding monetary policy has many dimensions. Does discretionary monetary policy tend to oscillate from excessive restraint to undue ease? Does the route to improved monetary performance lie in wiser use of discretion or greater reliance on rules? Should monetary policy be evaluated primarily in terms of the stock (or increase in the stock) of money and credit or of interest rates and credit conditions?

It is important to disentangle these questions. For example, a focus on interest rates or credit conditions should not be equated with discretionary policy. During and after the Second World War until the 1951 accord, the Federal Reserve pursued an essentially nondiscretionary automated monetary policy by pegging interest rates.

Paul Samuelson once reminded the Governors of the Federal Reserve that they were given two eyes so that they could watch both quantities and yields.[10] Clearly the Federal Reserve should, in executing discretionary monetary policy, use as guides and criteria the time path of money and other liquid assets as well as interest rates and credit conditions. In time of inflation, market interest rates are very hard to interpret because the price expectations built into the security markets are

10. Paul A. Samuelson, "Money, Interest Rates and Economic Activity: Their Interrelationship in a Market Economy," in American Bankers Association, *Proceedings of a Symposium on Money, Interest Rates and Economic Activity* (ABA, 1967), p. 44.

unknown. In a slowdown or recession, when credit demands sag, the Federal Reserve may overestimate its countercyclical contribution if the reduction in interest rates is taken as the measure of its shift toward ease. At least in the short run, however, a more quantity-oriented monetary policy is bound to mean less stability in interest rates. And that means more surprises and uncertainties for private borrowers and lenders, who are directly concerned about yields and credit conditions but only remotely with the behavior of aggregate quantities. Still this need not be a decisive consideration.

It takes, however, a big jump to go from the proposition that quantities deserve emphasis to the position that quantities alone should be the criteria of monetary policy. It is still another leap to the proposal that the only quantities that should count are those relating to one particular financial variable defined as money. Finally, one more giant step is required to conclude that an invariant growth rate of money provides the right rule for monetary policy.

That rule would mean that monetary policy could never be used to compensate for or neutralize shifts in fiscal policy or private demand. It would mean that interest rates, credit availability, nonmonetary flows such as those to thrift institutions, and the management of the federal debt could never enter directly into the determination of monetary policy. In my judgment, this puts blinders on the Federal Reserve—removing many important variables from its field of vision. Indeed, by sticking to a *rate-of-growth* target, the rule blinds the Fed even to the current *level* of the money supply. If the Federal Reserve missed the growth rate target for a time, the money supply would have departed from its desired growth track, but the Federal Reserve is told to resume the right rate of growth and not to restore the stock to a more normal relationship with gross national product.

Even then, the monetary rule offers the policy planner a quiet life only if he is prepared to believe that fiscal policy doesn't matter. What is most important and most dangerous about the monetary rule is its implicit precept: Ignore fiscal policy. Fortunately, nobody in a policy-making job takes that precept seriously. Consider the corollaries and you can understand its general rejection. For example, you must believe that the $25 billion deficit of fiscal 1968 had nothing to do with producing inflation. Many people seem willing to believe that fiscal policy is incapable of doing any good, but almost nobody can believe that it can do no harm. If fiscal policy is truly impotent, then obviously the surcharge can safely expire. But why stop there? Are we not being told that all taxes can be repealed so long as the Federal Reserve does its job? And can't we launch some important new social programs at the same time? Carried to its ultimate conclusions, the monetarist position would justify a totally unconstrained federal fiscal policy. Now I know a few people in Washington who would love an intellectual justification for fiscal irresponsibility. Some day they are going to discover the most important message of the monetarist view. And then we will see some fireworks.

The Dangers of Paralysis

Proposals for an inactive, inflexible, and fully automated economic policy reinforce the normal tendency for inertia to dominate Washington officials. This tendency reflects the simple fact of bureaucratic life that the exercise of good judgment is an extremely difficult and most unrewarding task. The penalty for errors of omission in Washington is not nearly so severe as that for errors of commission. Men who fail to take the stitch in time often manage to keep their jobs and sometimes even build reputations for being prudent and unflappable. Those who take action, however, are subject to intense public scrutiny of the wisdom and success of their decisions. It becomes tempting to the officials in charge of fiscal policy to pass the buck to the makers of monetary policy. And it becomes very tempting to the latter to allow themselves to be swept along by the tides of private demands for and supplies of credit. A bureaucracy tends to write its own laws of inertia in self-defense against public criticism.

The most important countervailing force against the threat

of bureaucratic paralysis is an alert and informed public opinion that insists on high standards of performance in economic policy. These standards have been transformed and greatly elevated during the 1960s. The American public has become a much tougher jury as a result of the interest in economic policy stimulated by the "new economics." Indeed, this may be the most important and most enduring contribution that the new economics has made.

Sometimes—especially in the view from public office—our citizens may appear to be unreasonably demanding and to display symptoms of hypochondria about minor shortfalls or excesses in the movement of business activity. And yet it becomes clear—particularly when one is no longer holding public office —that this widespread concern about economic performance is a vital antidote to complacency and bureaucratic inertia. It puts the spotlight on errors of omission as well as those of commission. The policy planners are obliged to strive for the best possible performance and to defend their decisions before the court of public opinion.

Passivity in economic policy is a meaningless objective. The only meaningful goal is stability in the growth of the economy. The important question is not how often the steering wheel is turned but how smoothly the car rides. "Look, Mom, no hands!" is not the formula for a smooth ride. That formula gave us a ride on the business cycle roller coaster for more than a century. Its rejection opened the way to an unprecedented period of prosperity in the sixties. Scrapping the activist strategy in economic policy would return us to the bumpy and unhappy performance of earlier times.

Improving Fiscal Procedures

We need to build on the activist foundation, not to undermine it. That requires the continuing effort at public education I have discussed previously. It also requires reform in our legislative procedures for implementing fiscal policy. A decade ago, the bipartisan and distinguished Commission on Money and

Credit displayed prophetic vision when it recommended that the Congress delegate to the President discretionary authority to raise and lower tax rates within specified amounts, in specified ways, subject to congressional veto.[11] A similar proposal —limited to tax reduction—was endorsed by President Kennedy in January 1962, but not a single congressman was sufficiently impressed to introduce it as a piece of legislation.

President Johnson pointed to a more modest reform in January 1965, suggesting that Congress might amend its own rules to assure that a prompt verdict—up or down—would be forthcoming in response to a presidential request for a change in tax rates for the purposes of economic stabilization. In his valedictory economic report, President Johnson again called for a change in legislative procedures to assure against fiscal stalemate. In addition, he proposed that Congress, in extending the surcharge, should give discretionary authority to his successor to eliminate the surcharge ahead of schedule should military or economic developments make that appropriate. I regret that President Nixon did not reiterate that request.

Congress appropriately treasures its consitutional prerogatives to alter our tax legislation. Given the repeated display of intense opposition to the delegation of authority, I am not optimistic about the near-term prospects for such a reform. But I believe that the active expression of informed opinion in favor of a delegation of authority to the President to vary tax rates is likely to improve congressional performance on fiscal policy. The experiences of 1967, 1968, and 1969 testify eloquently to the need for swift action in the face of inflationary dangers, and to the difficulties encountered by both President Johnson and President Nixon in getting congressional cooperation. Our legislators must face up to the challenge either by improving their record or by delegating authority to the President.

President Nixon, like President Johnson before him, has opposed overall congressional ceilings on federal expenditures. If

11. Report of the Commission on Money and Credit, *Money and Credit—Their Influence on Jobs, Prices, and Growth* (Englewood Cliffs, N.J.: Prentice-Hall, 1961), pp. 133–37.

Congress feels that the President's budget program calls for expenditures that are too large in any area, it should wield its knife in the appropriations process. But Congress should not shove a meat ax into the President's hands and insist that he chop the budget by a specified amount inconsistent with its own evaluation of individual appropriation requests.

If the present piecemeal appropriations process cannot work effectively to hold down total federal expenditures, then Congress should consider new and improved procedures. The basic requirement is that the sum of the parts emerging from the appropriations subcommittees should stay within bounds of a desirable total. Fulfilling this criterion should not be an insuperable task.

An Evolving Strategy

Procedural safeguards for prompt implementation of fiscal policy are important not because we need them frequently but rather because we need them badly on rare occasions. The shifts of gears required in recent years were associated with a spurt in defense spending. As long as defense spending continues to fluctuate markedly—in either direction—it will also continue to impose on us major and frequent shifts in other fiscal dimensions. If a significant demobilization occurs when peace arrives in Vietnam, then our economic policy planners will discover anew the difficulties of predicting and diagnosing the exact timing and pattern of defense changes, and of gauging the responses of businessmen and consumers to a shifting military situation. To sustain prosperity and to prevent a disruptive impact from the federal budget, policy makers will have to use their tools pragmatically and may have to put them to fairly frequent use. An economic policy of drift will not do when the tides shift in the defense area.

Quite apart from changes in defense spending, the setting of our fiscal and monetary dials will need to be altered from time to time. As we have seen, once an inflationary boom has taken hold, we need an unusually restrictive setting. But then we need to moderate the degree of restraint in timely fashion. Decisions of this nature have to rest on a pragmatic monitoring of the performance of the private economy, a diagnosis of its strengths and weaknesses, and on the best possible—although necessarily imperfect—forecast of its future performance. When its moments of truth come, economic policy must not be paralyzed.

If we can look beyond disinflation and demobilization, what type of stabilization policy can we envision for the long run? Experience suggests that, to promote a balance between overall supply and demand without inflation and without monetary restraint, the federal budget should normally generate a small surplus under conditions of full employment. Each presidential budget should focus on the full employment surplus that is being recommended as the key decision variable of fiscal policy.[12] It should explicitly state that the full employment surplus is being increased in order to provide restraint on aggregate demand (or more room for monetary ease); that it is being reduced for the reverse reasons; or that it is being held constant. That decision can be defended only on the basis of a forecast of aggregate demand, prices, and monetary and credit conditions. Such a procedure would not freeze the full employment surplus or search for a magic number; but it would place on the President the burden of proof for any shift in fiscal impact he would advocate.

Once the budget is submitted, Congress should review the proposed fiscal impact explicitly, approving or modifying the President's recommendation. Subsequent actions taken by the

12. As fiscal experts will recognize, the full employment surplus is an imperfect measure of budgetary impact. Three of its flaws are: (1) It sums and nets all types of expenditures and revenues as though they had equal bang-for-a-buck, which they don't; (2) it lags behind to the extent that government orders and contracts may influence private inventory investment (and employment demand) before they show up in the federal account; (3) it may show misleadingly large surpluses in a time of inflation if revenues respond more—and more promptly—to rising prices than do expenditures. We can adjust the full employment surplus for these to a degree, but we need better quantifications of fiscal impact. Still, for all its flaws, the full employment surplus is a shining jewel compared to the actual surplus (or deficit), which makes it appear that fiscal policy has shifted whenever a swing in private demand alters federal revenues.

Congress to modify the President's budget program should be monitored for their effect on the full employment surplus.

The desired full employment surplus can be achieved by various combinations of expenditure increases and tax changes. Decisions about this mix should be based primarily on social priorities rather than on stabilization considerations. A decision to cut taxes must be justified by the argument that the private needs that will thus be met by consumers and businesses are more urgent than the public needs that would be met by increasing federal programs. On the other hand, a proposal for increased taxes must rest on the view that social priorities call for federal outlays to grow more rapidly than private spending.

It would be a remarkable coincidence if, over the long run, society's priorities would call for no change in federal tax rates. Variations should be expected. Consideration of the appropriateness of tax rates should be a normal part of the budget program; indeed, if the President is not proposing any change, he should feel called upon to defend the optimality of existing tax rates.

The initial submission and the congressional review of the budgetary impact need not freeze decisions for the rest of the fiscal year. Obviously, the appropriations process and the legislative deliberation on tax proposals provide excellent opportunities to make marginal adjustments in the event of unanticipated developments in the private economy. But such adjustments should be made consciously and deliberately and should be significant only if there are major surprises.

Meanwhile, the Federal Reserve should have a quantitative, detailed flight plan, spelling out the path of money, bank credit, and other liquid assets, and the course of interest rates and credit conditions that would be expected to accompany a feasible and desirable path of economic activity, given the President's fiscal program. If the Federal Reserve intends to ease, the flight plan should register both above-normal growth of the key stocks and declining interest rates. Conversely, a policy of deliberate restraint should be reflected in both slowly growing quantities and rising yields.

As time passes, departures from the flight plan will be experienced. These must be carefully interpreted. For example, if quantities grow more rapidly and interest rates are higher than initially expected, demands for credit must have turned out to be stronger than was anticipated. The Fed must then decide whether these demands imply excessive economic expansion —which should be curbed—or whether they reflect an increased desire for liquidity that ought to be accommodated. When quantities, yields, or economic activity depart significantly from the flight plan, the Federal Reserve can and should respond, using the opportunities for small and frequent shifts in monetary policy.[13]

If the nation followed such fiscal and monetary procedures, we would grow to understand them and refine them over time. If we formed these habits, the government would be less likely to act as a major source of instability, and private decision makers might have less reason to alter their demands abruptly. We would also benefit over the long run from gradual improvements in forecasting techniques and increased accuracy in the assessment of the impact of policy actions. The strategy is not a counsel of perfection, nor a formula for achieving a neat exponential path of economic growth. But it is a route toward reduced instability. In this direction lies progress toward sustained prosperity as a normal state of affairs for the American economy.

The Uses of Prosperity

The bipartisan nature of our national commitment to full prosperity was clearly demonstrated in the initial months of the Nixon administration. This was the most significant and the most gratifying development in economic policy during 1969.

13. The process of adjustment I would envision is spelled out in James S. Duesenberry, "Tactics and Targets of Monetary Policy," in Federal Reserve Bank of Boston, *Controlling Monetary Aggregates,* Proceedings of the Monetary Conference, Nantucket Island, June 8–10, 1969 (FRB of Boston, 1969).

Full employment is worth preserving. To be sure, it has not solved all of the nation's social problems; indeed, it may have aggravated and exaggerated some by awakening unrealizable expectations of continued rapid progress.

It should be no surprise that national prosperity does not guarantee a happy society, any more than personal prosperity ensures a happy family. No growth of gross national product (GNP) can counter the tensions arising from an unpopular and unsuccessful war, a long overdue self-confrontation with conscience on racial injustice, a volcanic eruption of sexual mores, and an unprecedented assertion of independence by the young. Still, prosperity has changed our attitudes toward the vitality of the American economy, toward the usefulness of productive labor, toward our potentialities for continuing material progress; and it is a precondition for success in achieving many of our aspirations.

As Otto Eckstein once observed, ". . . When firing on all eight cylinders our economy is a mighty engine of social progress. . . ." [14] Prosperity growth has been the key to the reduction of the number of people below the statistical poverty line from 40 million in 1961 to 25 million in 1968. It has meant jobs for those formerly at the back of the hiring line. It has financed a revolution in the pension incomes and the health care of the aged. It has made economic security a reality to millions of middle-income families.

In retrospect, I wish that more of the fruits of growth had been devoted to the public sector. The quality and quantity of those services provided collectively have not kept pace with the growing abundance of the market baskets we buy at the supermarket and the department store. We have not made our cities safe or green or attractive. We have not gotten clean air or pure water. We have not provided the affluent with adequate and efficient airport facilities or the poor with reliable mass transit systems. We have not done enough to provide manpower train-

14. "Guideposts and the Prosperity of Our Day," in American Bankers Association, *Proceedings of a Symposium on Business-Government Relations* (ABA, 1966), p. 81.

ing and job opportunities for the poor or to offer adequate income support in the absence of jobs.

Realistically, the maintenance of high employment is a first condition for the achievement of these other objectives in the future. Only in a prosperous economy can our states and localities get the revenues they need to fulfill their social service obligations to rich and poor alike. Only in a prosperous economy with a firm labor market can manpower programs be successful in placing the disadvantaged.

Even with prosperity, the achievement of our social objectives represents an enormous task for the years ahead. But it is enormous because it strains our will and determination, not because it strains our resources. We have the material requirements to deal effectively with these problems.

Take poverty as the outstanding example. If it were possible to identify all the people whose incomes are below the statistical poverty line in the United States today and simply to hand them enough dollars to raise their incomes to the line, it would take only $10 billion a year to eliminate poverty. That is the size of the poverty gap—only 1 percent of our gross national product. I must hasten to add a number of qualifications. In the first place, the statistical poverty line—about $3,500 a year for a family of four—is still a pretty meager standard of living. Second, antipoverty dollars cannot be spent in a pinpointed way that would put each and every cent into the poverty gap; some of the benefits of job programs and cash assistance will seep above the poverty line. Yet the size of the gap is a reminder that the cost of eliminating poverty in our society is within our grasp, if we are prepared to devote our resources to it.

How much can we afford to spend on increased efforts to eliminate poverty? My first inclination is to respond to that question with another question: How long can we afford to tolerate poverty in an affluent society? A less rhetorical answer is that we can afford anything that we want so strongly that we are willing to pay for it through higher taxes.

If the nation were willing to return to the average income tax rates that prevailed from 1954 to 1961, we could have roughly $25 billion a year more to spend on social programs than with the tax rates now in prospect for the early seventies. If our combined federal, state, and local taxes as a percentage of GNP matched the average of the major Western European countries, we would have about $40 billion to $50 billion more a year in government revenues.[15] Then we could have more public-sector butter by sacrificing some private-sector butter. Instead, we see a tax-cut bandwagon rolling; and we are obliged to fight a defensive battle merely to keep federal revenues from being further eroded after the expiration of the surcharge.

If we can hold the line on taxes, how much and how fast we move toward our social goals at home will be determined largely by the size of the defense budget. If this is a fact of political life, it reflects an absurdity. By any standard of logic, an increase or decrease in defense spending amounting to 1 percent of our GNP should have no significant effect on the amount of our spending on social programs at home.

National defense is an overhead cost of our society, and we should want to share overheads fairly. If 1 percent of our GNP floated out to sea and we were asked how to share the loss equitably, no one would suggest that our federal civilian programs ought to bear the major share of the burden. If we thought that the initial allocation between private and public civilian outlays was about right, we might want to share the costs of extra defense proportionately, as I noted in Chapter 3. That would impose about 15 percent on public nondefense expenditures and 85 percent on private outlays. If we felt that the federal civilian outlays had particularly high priority, we might want to exempt them.

15. For 1966, U.S. taxes were 28.1 percent of GNP. The figure for France was 38.6 percent; for West Germany, 34.9 percent; for the United Kingdom, 31.3 percent; for Italy, 29.1 percent. A simple arithmetic average of the four European ratios is 33.5 percent, or 5.4 percentage points higher than the U.S. figure. Applying that to 1969 GNP, the result is $50 billion. The statistics on taxes as a percent of GNP are from David B. Perry, "The Burden of Taxation—International Comparisons," *Canadian Tax Journal*, Vol. 17 (May–June 1969), p. 208.

The absurd battle between defense and the cities arises because we insist on rather stable tax rates and hence on a relatively constant federal share of our national product. Thus defense and nondefense programs are plunged into a direct tug-of-war for a fixed volume of budgetary resources. This is surely the greatest paradox of resource allocation in our society. Defense spending—with its 9 percent of GNP—is pitted against nondefense federal, state, and local expenditures—with their 14 percent of GNP—while the big 77 percent of our GNP that goes into private spending remains a bystander. And because controllable federal civilian spending is concentrated in aid to cities and the poor, the bulk of the pressure is exerted on about 5 percent of our GNP. When defense goes down, efforts to assist the cities and the poor can go up. When defense goes up, we seem to expect the belt-tightening to be concentrated in these social programs.

The paradox works both ways. In the fiscal years 1964 and 1965, the declining defense budget was a key catalyst in producing Lyndon Johnson's magic compound of great new social programs, tax cuts, and tight control on the total of the federal budget. Once the Vietnam buildup began, however, the same paradox squeezed nondefense spending and yet generated complaints about reckless government civilian spending.

This paradox of allocation has social as well as economic consequences. It is, I submit, no coincidence that the leaders of the civil rights movement were among the earliest opponents of the Vietnam war. It is no coincidence that the attack on the "military-industrial complex" is being led by the proponents of increased social efforts.

Appropriately, the threat of holocaust in our cities as a result of internal strife and injustice is being recognized as a greater and more disturbing danger than that of nuclear holocaust. Appropriately, the Congress is casting a critical eye on the efficiency of defense programs in order to free resources for fighting the battle on the home front for a united society. Appropriately, after our sad experience in Vietnam, the judgments of military experts in uniform are no longer sacrosanct. The

claims of the Joint Chiefs of Staff on resources are no longer
viewed as absolutes any more than are the claims of the Commissioner of Education. The halos are coming off the military.

But the halos should not be replaced with horns. The military-industrial complex is no worse—as well as no better—than
most of the interest groups that operate legitimately in our
pluralistic system. To be sure, business firms with products to
sell the Defense Department are enthusiastic—sometimes over-
enthusiastic—about their merchandise, and so are business
firms which sell products to the Bureau of Public Roads and the
Department of Housing and Urban Development. Of course,
generals want to be certain—perhaps too certain—that they
have the manpower and the equipment to do their job, and so
do the Director of the Office of Economic Opportunity and the
Commissioner of Education. There is as much of a "socio-
urban complex" as a military-industrial complex in our society,
and we need both. The trouble with our past record lies in the
way public opinion and political procedures have elevated the
military-industrial group to a sanctified position. It is not that
they have behaved worse than other groups, but that they have
been treated so much better.

It would be bad economics and bad politics for our national
defense effort to be cast as the villain barring progress on the
home front. And it would be bad economics and bad politics for
enthusiasts about full economic opportunity and urban development—among whom I include myself—to oppose *automatically*
any new expenditures for national defense. Such proposals
should be judged on their true contribution to our national
security. If some pass that test, we can afford them *and* greater
social efforts at home.

I have no fundamental solution for this political problem.
But I do have one suggestion which could help give us a more
rational, calm determination of the military budget of our nation, at least for the next few years. The existence of the tax
surcharge enables us to balance changes in the military budget
against private-sector butter rather than against public-sector

butter. If we decide that some extra defense programs are essential, let us pay for them through taxes rather than by squeezing federal nondefense programs. And let us distribute the benefits of deep cuts in defense spending through tax reductions.

This requires that we decide in advance as a nation how much we will channel into priority social programs. Given the urgency of our social needs, it would seem essential—indeed, too modest for my own preferences—to earmark the full fiscal dividend resulting from economic growth for public civilian uses. That annual increment of about $15 billion would have to finance some built-in general increases in federal workloads, and it would have to be guarded against proposals for expanding public works and subsidy programs that are not at the top of society's priority list. It would then give us elbow room for manpower training and job programs, income maintenance, education, health, and urban development, and for revenue-sharing with states and localities.

Once the decision is made to put the fiscal dividend to public civilian use, the level of tax rates must be geared to the size of the military budget in order to maintain a responsible fiscal policy. Barring surprises in private demand that might call for a particularly restrictive or stimulative fiscal policy for reasons of economic stabilization, we should want the tax surcharge to be gradually phased out as defense spending declines below its current $80 billion level. Algebraically, we would want alterations in the surcharge revenues to approximate the difference between $80 billion and defense spending. The surcharge, which now yields about $12 billion, would drop to zero when defense outlays were reduced to $68 billion. If, on the other hand, defense spending requirements exceeded $80 billion, the surcharge would be raised above 10 percent.

This procedure would change the nature of the tradeoff by bringing private expenditures into the picture. Taxpayers would recognize that decisions to increase or decrease defense spending would mean decisions to live with higher taxes or to lower

them. We would reduce the intolerable pressures on our social
efforts and end the absurd pitched battle between internal
social welfare and external national security.

Summary

A quick glance at the agenda for future economic policy
points to three categories of problem areas: extending our
prosperity, reconciling it with price stability, and channeling its
dividends into the areas of highest priority.

The economic breakthrough in the sixties came in the
achievement of prosperity as the normal state of affairs in the
American economy. The continuation of that success rests upon
conveying some new lessons to the American public as part of
its education in economic policy, reforming our legislative
procedures for implementing fiscal policy, and—most of all—
maintaining vigilance and flexibility in translating good judgment into policy action.

The task of combining prosperity with price stability now
stands as the major unsolved problem of aggregative economic
performance. During the coming decade we must find a satisfactory compromise that yields growth and unemployment rates
that we can be proud of, on the one hand, and a price performance that we can be comfortable with, on the other. It will
take time to find that compromise; for once, we have the
prospect of sufficiently durable prosperity to give us the opportunity to probe and test and learn from experience. Monetary and fiscal policy alone are unlikely to deliver a satisfactory
compromise; they will need to be reinforced and supported by
other public policies and by private efforts to improve the workings of all our institutions.

The key priority items on the nation's shopping list seem to
lie increasingly in areas that have traditionally been in the public
sector. Perhaps we can, as President Nixon hopes, enlist more
private effort to serve these public purposes. But, regardless of
who pays the bill, we cannot expect to obtain at bargain prices
green, safe, and attractive cities; quality and equality in educa-

tional opportunities; or a realization of the Employment Act's objective of "useful employment opportunities . . . for those able, willing, and seeking to work. . . ." [16] Perhaps the nation will finally learn to appreciate Justice Holmes's dictum that "taxes are what we pay for civilized society. . . ." [17] That is the only way we can really hope to achieve our goals.

All of these objectives are linked with the continuation of prosperity. It is sometimes said that the President has a great incentive to end the war in Vietnam soon, for if it lasts much longer it will become Nixon's war as well as Johnson's war. It can equally well be said that the President has a great incentive to continue our prosperity, for if it lasts much longer it will become Nixon's prosperity as well as Johnson's prosperity. Americans of all political persuasions should be glad to see the credit shared in a bipartisan way.

16. 60 Stat. 23.
17. *Compania General de Tabacos de Filipinas* v. *Collector of Internal Revenue*, 275 U.S. 100 (1927).

appendix

Potential GNP: Its Measurement and Significance[1]

Potential GNP and Policy

"How much output can the economy produce under conditions of full employment?" The concept and measurement of potential GNP are addressed to this question. It is a question with policy significance because the pursuit of full employment (or "maximum employment" in the language of the Employment Act) is a goal of policy. And a target of full employment of labor needs to be linked to a corresponding target of full employment output, since policy measures designed to influence employment operate by affecting aggregate demand and production. How far we stand from the target of full employment output is important information in formulating fiscal and monetary policy. Thus, quantification of potential output offers one of the guides to stabilization policy and one indicator of its success.

The quantification of potential output—and the accompanying measure of the "gap" between actual and potential—is at best an uncertain estimate and not a firm, precise measure. While there are more precise measures of economic performance, they are not fully substitutable for the concept of potential output. To appraise the vigor of an expanding economy, it is important and enlightening to study customary cyclical measures, such as advance over previous peak levels or advance over recession trough levels. But these measures do not tell us how far we have to go to meet our targets, unless we are prepared to assume that each peak is like any other one and all troughs are likewise uniform. The record of the past decade testifies to the dramatic differences among cyclical peaks in levels of resource utilization.

The evaluation of potential output can also help to point up the

1. Reprinted, with slight changes, from American Statistical Association, *Proceedings of the Business and Economic Statistics Section* (1962).

132

enormous social cost of idle resources. If programs to lower unemployment from 5½ to 4 percent of the labor force are viewed as attempts to raise the economy's "grade" from 94½ to 96, the case for them may not seem compelling. Focus on the gap helps to remind policymakers of the large reward associated with such an improvement.

The 4 Percent Unemployment Rate

Potential GNP is a supply concept, a measure of productive capacity. But it is not a measure of how much output could be generated by unlimited amounts of aggregate demand. The nation would probably be most productive in the short run with inflationary pressure pushing the economy. But the social target of maximum production and employment is constrained by a social desire for price stability and free markets. The full employment goal must be understood as striving for maximum production without inflationary pressure; or, more precisely, as aiming for a point of balance between more output and greater stability, with appropriate regard for the social valuation of these two objectives.

It is interesting and perhaps surprising that there seems to be more agreement that a 4 percent unemployment rate is a reasonable target under existing labor market conditions than on any of the analytical steps needed to justify such a conclusion. Economists have never developed a clear criterion of tolerable price behavior or any quantitative balancing of conflicting objectives which could be invoked either to support or attack the target of a 4 percent rate. Indeed, I should expect that many economists who agree on the 4 percent target would disagree in estimating how prices and wages would behave if we were on target. Nor can the 4 percent rate be said to meet Beveridge's criterion for full employment—that job vacancies should be equal to the number of unemployed. We simply have no count of job vacancies and could not possibly translate Beveridge's goal into any available measure of unemployment.

Having said what the 4 percent unemployment rate is not, I shall now state that it is the target rate of labor utilization underlying the calculation of potential GNP in this paper. The statistical and methodological problems would not be altered if a different rate were selected; only the numbers would be changed.

Potential GNP as a Short-run Concept

In estimating potential GNP, most of the facts about the economy are taken as they exist: technological knowledge, the capital stock, natural resources, the skill and education of the labor force are all data, rather than variables. Potential differs from actual only because the potential concept depends on the assumption—normally contrary to fact—that aggregate demand is exactly at the level that yields a rate of unemployment equal to 4 percent of the civilian labor force. If, in fact, aggregate demand is lower, part of potential GNP is not produced; there is unrealized potential or a gap between actual and potential output.

The failure to use one year's potential fully can influence future potential GNP: To the extent that low utilization rates and accompanying low profits and personal incomes hold down investment in plant, equipment, research, housing, and education, the growth of potential GNP will be retarded. Because today's actual output influences tomorrow's productive capacity, success in the stabilization objective promotes more rapid economic growth.

The Measurement Problem

As it has been defined above, potential output is observed only when the unemployment rate is 4 percent, and even then must be viewed as subject to stochastic variation. At any other time, it must be regarded as a hypothetical magnitude. The observed actual measures of labor utilization tell us by a simple arithmetic calculation how much employment would have to increase, given the labor force, to make the unemployment rate 4 percent. But they do not offer similar direct information on other matters that might make labor input at full employment different from its observed level: (a) how average hours worked per man would be altered if the level of aggregate demand were consistent with full employment; (b) how participation rates in the labor force—and hence the size of the labor force—would be affected under conditions of full employment.

Nor do the actual data reveal directly what aggregate labor productivity would be under full employment conditions. There are many reasons why productivity might be altered in the aggregate: The added workers, changed average hours, possible alterations in the sectoral distribution of employment, higher utilization rate of capital, and altered efficiency in the use of employees all could make a difference in productivity at full employment.

The Leap from Unemployment to Output

Ideally, the measurement of potential output would appraise the various possible influences of high employment on labor input and productivity and evaluate the influences step by step, developing quantitative estimates for each adjustment to produce the desired measure of potential. While I shall discuss the steps individually below, the basic technique I am reporting consists of a leap from the unemployment rate to potential output rather than a series of steps involving the several underlying factors. Strictly speaking, the leap requires the assumption that, whatever the influence of slack economic activity on average hours, labor force participation, and manhour productivity, the magnitudes of all these effects are related to the unemployment rate. With this assumption, the unemployment rate can be viewed as a proxy variable for all the ways in which output is affected by idle resources. The measurement of potential output then is simplified into an estimate of how much output is depressed by unemployment in excess of 4 percent.

Statistical Estimates

The answer I have to offer is simple and direct. In the postwar period, on the average, each extra percentage point in the unemployment rate above 4 percent has been associated with about a 3 percent decrement in real GNP. This result emerged from three methods of relating output to the unemployment rate.

First differences. In one technique, quarterly changes in the unemployment rate (Y), expressed in percentage points, are related to quarterly percentage changes in real GNP (X). This regression equation, fitted to fifty-five quarterly observations from 1947-II to 1960-IV, yields:

$$Y = 0.30 - 0.30X \qquad (r = 0.79).$$

According to this estimate, the unemployment rate will rise by 0.3 point from one quarter to the next if real GNP is unchanged, as secular gains in productivity and growth in the labor force push up the unemployment rate. For each extra 1 percent of GNP, unem-

136 *The Political Economy of Prosperity*

ployment is 0.3 point lower. At any point in time, taking previous quarters as given, 1 percentage point more in the unemployment rate means 3.3 percent less GNP.

Trial gaps. A second method consists of selecting and testing certain exponential paths of potential output, using alternative assumed growth rates and benchmark levels. The percentage gaps implied by these paths are then related to the unemployment rate (U) using a regression equation: $U = a + b$ (gap). The criteria for judging the validity of the assumed potential paths are: (1) goodness of fit; (2) absence of any trend in the residuals; (3) agreement with the principle that potential GNP should equal actual GNP when $U = 4$.

The slope terms in this equation fitted to various paths and different periods consistently ran from 0.28 up to 0.38. One such equation was reported in the March 1961 statement of the Council of Economic Advisers to the Joint Economic Committee. It was:

$$U = 3.72 + 0.36 \text{ (gap)} \qquad (r = 0.93)$$

where the gap was derived from a 3½ percent trend line through actual real GNP in mid-1955. The equation was fitted to quarterly data for 1953–60. It implies that an increment of unemployment of 1 percent is associated with an output loss equal to 2.8 percent of potential output—or a somewhat larger percentage of *actual* output when actual is below potential. The estimated unemployment rate associated with a zero gap is 3.72 percent, not too far from the 4.0 percent ideal.

Fitted trend and elasticity. The first method described above relied on the use of *changes* in GNP and in unemployment. The second method used *levels* but assumed the trend of output growth at constant unemployment rates. It is also possible to derive the output-unemployment coefficient from data on levels without assuming a trend. The following model permits such a calculation:

There is a constant elasticity relationship in the relevant range between the ratio of actual (A) to potential (P) output, on the one hand, and the employment rate ($N=100-U$) as a fraction of its potential level (N_F):

$$N/N_F = (A/P)^a.$$

There is a constant growth rate (r) of potential output starting from some level (P_0) such that at any time (t):

$$P_t = P_0 \exp(rt).$$

By substitution and rearrangement:

$$N_t = [A_t^a N_F] / [P_0^a \exp(art)];$$

logarithmically:

$$\log N_t = \log (N_F/P_0^a) + a \log A_t - art.$$

The log of the employment rate is here related to a time trend and to the log of actual real GNP. When a regression equation is fitted to $\log N$ as the dependent variable and $\log A$ and t as independent variables: (1) the coefficient of $\log A$ is the "output elasticity of the employment rate"; (2) the coefficient of time is the product of that elasticity and the potential growth rate, and therefore yields an estimate of the potential growth rate; and (3) the intercept yields the benchmark (P_0) for any given N_F, here taken as 96.

Fitted to varying sample periods, the estimated elasticity coefficient ran 0.35 to 0.40, suggesting that each 1 percentage point reduction in unemployment means slightly less than a 3 percent increment in output (near the potential level). The trend growth rate, fitted to 1947–60 quarterly data, was 3.9 percent, but it was clear that this was not uniform throughout the period. For the post-Korean period, the estimated trend growth in potential was near 3½ percent, while for the 1947–53 period, it was near 4½ percent.

The uniformity that emerged from these various techniques was the approximate 3-to-1 link between output and the unemployment rate. My own subjectively weighted average of the relevant coefficients is 3.2, yielding the following estimate of potential:

$$P = A [1 + 0.032 (U - 4)].$$

When the unemployment rate is 4 percent, potential GNP is estimated as equal to actual; at a 5 percent rate of unemployment, the estimated gap is 3.2 percent of GNP. In the periods from which this relationship was obtained the unemployment rate varied from about 3 to 7½ percent; the relation is not meant to be extrapolated outside this range. I have no reason to expect the 3.2 coefficient to apply if unemployment were either 1 or 15 percent of the labor force.

Smoothing the Potential Path

The implied time-series of potential GNP derived by applying the 3.2 coefficient to excess unemployment for the period 1954 to date would be a curve that wiggles from quarter to quarter, even dipping at times. The dips and small increases in estimated potential are concentrated in advanced stages of expansion—1956–57, 1959, and early 1962. Quarters of rapid rise in estimated potential output occur in early expansion—1955, 1958, 1961.

The question that arises is whether (1) these wiggles and jiggles should be taken seriously, as indications of irregular or cyclical patterns in the growth of productive capacity or (2) whether they should be attributed to an imperfect correlation of the unemployment rate with unused potential output. In the former case, the irregular path upward would be the estimated series of potential GNP. In the latter case, some smoothing of that irregular path would be in order.

One way of smoothing which eliminates all the ripples is to substitute a simple exponential curve that corresponds with the trend and level of the wiggly series. Such a line is obtained by a trend that goes through actual output in mid-1955 as a benchmark and moves upward at a 3½ percent annual rate. The trend measure of potential presents an opposite extreme alternative to the implied wiggly path mentioned above—the view that the upward path of potential GNP has been perfectly smooth in the post-Korean period. On the whole, the two measures agree quite well. A trend line with either a 3 or a 4 percent growth rate—or with a markedly different benchmark level—would not fit equally well. In general, periods of early expansion—like 1955; 1958-II to 1959-I; and 1961-II to 1961-IV —show larger gaps by the unemployment measure than by the trend technique. The reverse is true for late expansion and recession periods, like 1956-II to 1958-I and 1959-III to 1961-I.

My own inclination is to select the smooth trend measure of potential output for the post-Korean period. I find it difficult to accept the verdict that potential output has actually contracted at times, as the unsmoothed unemployment measure implies. Nor can I believe that the economy's *productive capacity* rises most rapidly in early expansion, even though actual production may be increasing briskly. This is not the period when investment expenditures—much less completed investment projects—are at a peak; nor is it a time of heavy innovations, by any external evidence I know.

The spurts shown in early expansion periods can be accounted for by the hypothesis that unemployment lags somewhat behind the movement of output, and therefore is slow to decline in early recovery. Indeed, in statistical tests of some of the regression equations reported above, it was found that unemployment in the current quarter depends on past as well as current levels of GNP, with a higher level of past output meaning less current unemployment. This implies that decisions on hiring labor for next quarter are strengthened by a high level of current output.

The cyclical ripples in the unemployment measure may also reflect, in part, a lead of the workweek in advance of employment. Total manhours worked rise more rapidly than employment in early expansion and less rapidly in late expansion. The initial impact of a change in the pace of economic activity is particularly strong on the workweek and is later shifted more fully onto employment. Presumably, this lagged effect might be incorporated into the estimate of potential based on the unemployment rate, in such a way as to smooth that potential curve and bring it closer to the trend estimate of potential. But, for the post-Korean period, there is no obvious shift in the trend of potential; and the 3½ percent trend line, while obviously too smooth a time path, fills the assignment rather well.

The trend estimate of potential for the 1954–62 period still rests on the unemployment-output relationship reviewed above, that an excess of 1 point in the unemployment rate means, on the average, a loss of about 3 percent in output. The trend line, however, suggests that the output loss per point of the unemployment rate exceeds 3 percent in late expansion and in recession and is somewhat less than 3 percent in early expansion.

It should be noted that this trend does not fit the earlier postwar years. If one projected the 3½ percent trend back to 1947, the trend technique would clearly overestimate potential output. The indicated potential growth of the 1947–53 period is nearer to 4½ percent. The lower potential growth rate of the post-Korean period is associated, in part, with less success in making full use of our potential. The gaps between potential and actual have held down the size and held up the average age of our capital stock, thereby lowering the growth of potential.

The Steps

The findings above assert that a reduction in unemployment, measured as a percentage of the labor force, has a much larger than proportionate effect on output. To appraise and evaluate this finding, it is necessary to inspect the steps which were leaped over in the statistical relationships between output and unemployment. Clearly, the simple addition of 1 percent of a given labor force to the ranks of the employed would increase employment by only slightly more than 1 percent: $100/(100 - U)$ percent to be exact. If the work-week and productivity were unchanged, the increment to output would be only that $1+$ percent. The 3 percent result implies that considerable output gains in a period of rising utilization rates must stem from some or all of the following: induced increases in the size of the labor force; longer average weekly hours; and greater productivity.

Labor Force

Participation in the labor force as we measure it consists of either having a job or seeking actively to work. The resulting measures of labor force are not pure reflections of supply; they are affected by job availability. In a slack labor market, people without a job may give up when they are convinced that job-hunting is a hopeless pursuit. They then may be viewed as having left the labor force though they stand ready and eager to work. Furthermore, there are secondary or passive members of the labor force who will not actively seek employment but would accept gainful employment if a job came looking for them. This latter group suffers little or no personal hardship in not having work, but the output they would contribute in a fully employed economy is a relevant part of the nation's potential GNP.

There may be induced changes in the labor force in the opposite direction: For example, the loss of a job by the breadwinner of a family might increase the measured labor force by leading his wife and teenage children to seek work. The prewar literature debated the probable net effects of these opposing influences on participation rates. However, the postwar record has convincingly delivered the verdict that a weak labor market depresses the size of the labor force. But the magnitude and timing of the effect is not clear.

Even the conceptual problem of defining a potential labor force is difficult—we should not wish to count only the secondary labor force members who would appear for work tomorrow morning; on the other hand, we would not want to include all those who might be attracted by many years of continued job availability. The response of participation rates is likely to be a complicated lagged phenomenon which will not be closely tied to the current unemployment rate. While this aspect of the difference between potential and actual output is hard to quantify, zero is certainly not a satisfactory estimate. At the end of 1960, the Bureau of Labor Statistics estimated the difference between actual and "normal" labor force at 561,000. If this figure is taken as the induced effect of poor opportunities for jobs, it implies that, in those recession conditions, for every ten people listed as unemployed over and above the 4 percent rate, there were three additional potential workers who were not actively seeking work.

Hours

Taking into account the normal secular decline in hours worked per man, there is a clear relationship between movements in average hours and in output. When output has been rising rapidly, average hours have expanded—or, at least, have not contracted. On the other hand, periods of low growth or decline in GNP mean more rapid declines in average hours per man. The data point toward the concept of a full employment path of average annual hours. But the concept of full employment hours is hard to quantify: For example, in a rapid rise of output toward full employment, the amount of overtime might well push the workweek above the level consistent with steady full employment. Furthermore, economy-wide data on average hours are notoriously poor. However, using what evidence is available, we find that each 1 percent difference in output is associated with a difference of 0.14 percent in hours per man, including both overtime and part-time work.

The figure of 0.14 is obtained by fitting a least-squares regression line to annual data for 1947–59. The data are found in the Bureau of Labor Statistics Release (USDL-4155), of June 28,

1960. The variables are percent change in manhours of work per person employed (Y) and percent change in private nonagricultural output (X), restricted to private nonagricultural output and employment; establishment figures are the source of the manhour estimates. The fitted line is:

$$Y = 0.843 + 0.142X \qquad (r = 0.85).$$

When this equation is used to compare average hours for different possible outputs at the same point in time, the 0.142 coefficient reflects the percentage difference in hours per man that accompanies a 1 percent difference in output.

Returning to the finding that a 1 percentage point reduction in the unemployment rate means 3.2 percent more GNP, the hours-output estimate above indicates that it will also be accompanied by an increase of nearly 0.5 percent in hours per man, or an addition of about 0.2 of an hour to the workweek. With an allowance for induced gains in labor force, based illustratively on the 1960 estimate cited above, the reduction of 1 point in the unemployment rate means perhaps a 1.8 percent increase in total labor input measured in manhours. Then, to get the 3.2 percent increment in output, manhour productivity must rise by about 1.4 percent.

Productivity

The direct checks that could be made on productivity data were consistent with this implication of the output-unemployment relationship. The record clearly shows that manhour productivity is depressed by low levels of utilization, and that periods of movement toward full employment yield considerably above-average productivity gains.

The implications and explanations of this phenomenon are intriguing. Indeed, many a priori arguments have been made for the reverse view—that depressed levels of activity will stimulate productivity through pressure on management to cut costs, through a weeding-out of inefficient firms and low quality workers, and through availability of more and higher quality capital per worker for those employees who retain their jobs. If such effects exist, the empirical record demonstrates that they are swamped by other forces working in the opposite direction.

I have little direct evidence to offer on the mechanism by which low levels of utilization depress productivity. I can offer some speculation and try to encourage other researchers to pursue this problem with concrete evidence at a microeconomic level. The positive relationship between output and labor productivity suggests that much of labor input is essentially a fixed cost for fairly substantial periods. Thus high output levels permit the spreading of labor overheads, and low production levels raise unit fixed costs of labor. At times, we may take too seriously our textbook examples which view labor as a variable factor, with only capital costs as fixed. Even the most casual empiricism points to an overhead component in labor costs. There are many reasons why employment may not be easily variable:

Contractual commitments may tie the hand of management in a downward direction—employees may have guaranteed annual wages, supplementary unemployment compensation, rights to severence pay, and so forth, as well as actual contracts for a term of employment.

Technological factors, in a broad sense, may also be important. A firm plans on a division of labor and degree of specialization attuned to "normal" operations. If operations fall below normal, there may be marked indivisibilities which prevent the firm from curtailing its employment of specialists, clerical and sales personnel, and supervisors in parallel with its cutback in output.

Transactions costs associated with laying off labor and then, in the future, doing new hiring may be another influence retarding the adjustment of labor input to fluctuations in sales and output.

Acquired skills that existing employees have learned on the job may make them particularly valuable to the firm so that it pays to stockpile underemployed labor rather than run the risk of having to hire untrained men when business conditions improve.

Morale factors may also make layoffs undesirable.

All of these factors could help explain why slack economic activity is accompanied by "on-the-job underemployment," reflected in depressed levels of manhour productivity. Firms obviously do lay off labor in recession but they do so reluctantly. Their problems may be mitigated, in part, by the presence of voluntary quits which permit a downward adjustment of employment without layoffs. In part, the impact of slack on manhour productivity may be reduced by shortening average hours to spread the work and the wage bill without a cut in employment. But these appear to be only partial offsets.

To the extent that the productivity losses of recessions are associated with fixity of labor costs, they would not be maintained indefinitely. If the recession was of long duration—or merely was expected to last a long time—firms would adjust their employment more drastically. On this reasoning, in an era when business cycle dips are continually short and mild, one might expect productivity to bear more of the brunt of recession and labor input to be less affected, even relative to the decline in output.

Changes in the level of economic activity are associated with shifts in the composition of employment and output by industry. A slack economy is accompanied by particularly depressed output in durable goods manufacturing industries, where output per manhour is especially high. My own intuition suggested that this might be an important explanation of the relationship between productivity and the unemployment rate. But calculations on the change in composition from recession to recovery years indicate that, while shifts in industrial composition do influence aggregate productivity in the expected direction, the magnitude of the effect is trivial. There is some significance to the compositional shift between agriculture and nonagricultural industries. Manhour input in agriculture seems to be independent of overall economic activity in the short run, so all variations in labor input can be regarded as occurring in the nonagricultural sector. I assumed illustratively above that a point reduction in the unemployment rate means an increase in total manhours of 1.8 percent. If all of that 1.8 percent goes into nonagriculture, this would add 0.1 percent to economywide productivity (for given levels of productivity in each sector). This is still only a minor part of the total productivity gain that accompanies reduced unemployment.

Thus far, I have ignored the dependence of labor productivity on plant and equipment capacity. The entire discussion of potential output in this paper has, in effect, assumed that idle labor is a satisfactory measure of all idle resources. In fact, measures of excess capacity in industrial plant and equipment do show a close relationship to unemployment—idle men are accompanied by idle machines. But the correlation is not perfect and operating rates in industry should be considered along with employment data as an indicator of the gap between potential and actual output. Obviously, if capital were fully employed while there was much unemployed labor, this would hold down the productivity gains that could be obtained through full employment of labor. Robert Solow did use capital stock data together with unemployment data in fitting a production function for 1929 to date (see the *American Economic Review* of May 1962). His estimates of potential output for the post-Korean period agreed remarkably well with those I am reporting.

Still, I shall feel much more satisfied with the estimation of potential output when our data and our analysis have advanced to the point where the estimation can proceed step by step and where the capital factor can be explicitly taken into account. Meanwhile, the measure of potential must be used with care. The trend line yields a point-estimate of the gap, for example, $31.3 billion for 1962-II. But that specific figure must be understood as the center of a range of plausible estimates. By my personal evaluation of its degree of accuracy, I find potential output useful—and superior to substitute concepts—for many analytical purposes.

selected bibliography on money and interest

The following articles report empirical results showing a negative relation between the demand for money and the rate of interest:

Bronfenbrenner, Martin, and Thomas Mayer. "Liquidity Functions in the American Economy," *Econometrica,* Vol. 28 (October 1960), pp. 810–34.

Brown, Arthur J. "Interest, Prices, and the Demand Schedule for Idle Money," *Oxford Economic Papers,* No. 2 (May 1939), pp. 46–69.

Brunner, Karl, and Allan H. Meltzer. "Some Further Investigations of Demand and Supply Functions for Money," *Journal of Finance,* Vol. 19 (May 1964), pp. 240–83.

Chow, Gregory C. "On the Long-run and Short-run Demand for Money," *Journal of Political Economy,* Vol. 74 (April 1966), pp. 111–31.

Courchene, T. J., and H. T. Shapiro. "The Demand for Money: A Note from the Time Series," *Journal of Political Economy,* Vol. 72 (October 1964), pp. 498–503.

de Leeuw, Frank. "The Demand for Money: Speed of Adjustment, Interest Rates, and Wealth," in George Horwich (ed.), *Monetary Process and Policy: A Symposium* (Homewood, Illinois: Richard D. Irwin, 1967), pp. 167–86.

Eisner, Robert. "Another Look at Liquidity Preference," *Econometrica,* Vol. 31 (July 1963), pp. 531–38.

Hamburger, Michael J. "The Demand for Money by Households, Money Substitutes, and Monetary Policy," *Journal of Political Economy,* Vol. 74 (December 1966), pp. 600–23.

Heller, H. R. "The Demand for Money: The Evidence from the Short-run Data," *Quarterly Journal of Economics,* Vol. 79 (May 1965), pp. 291–303.

Kalecki, Michal. "The Short-term Rate of Interest and the Velocity of Cash Circulation," *Review of Economic Statistics,* Vol. 23 (May 1941), pp. 97–99.

Khusro, A. M. "An Investigation of Liquidity Preference," *Yorkshire Bulletin of Economic and Social Research,* Vol. 4 (January 1952), pp. 1–20.

Laidler, David. "Some Evidence on the Demand for Money," *Journal of Political Economy,* Vol. 74 (February 1966), pp. 55–68.

————. "The Rate of Interest and the Demand for Money—Some Empirical Evidence," *Journal of Political Economy,* Vol. 74 (December 1966), pp. 543–55.

146

Selected Bibliography 147

1954), pp. 456–60.

445–49.

Vol. 57 (December 1967), pp. 1168–81.

(September 1966), pp. 441–57.

(September 1967), pp. 405–18.

Vol. 22 (March 1967), pp. 71–76.

(October 1964), pp. 476–509.

Economic Statistics, Vol. 29 (May 1947), pp. 124–31.

314–17.

Selected Bibliography 147

Latané, Henry A. "Cash Balances and the Interest Rate—A Pragmatic Approach," *Review of Economics and Statistics,* Vol. 36 (November 1954), pp. 456–60.

_____. "Income Velocity and Interest Rates: A Pragmatic Approach," *Review of Economics and Statistics,* Vol. 42 (November 1960), pp. 445–49.

Lee, Tong Hun. "Alternative Interest Rates and the Demand for Money: The Empirical Evidence," *American Economic Review,* Vol. 57 (December 1967), pp. 1168–81.

_____. "Substitutability of Non-Bank Intermediary Liabilities for Money: The Empirical Evidence," *Journal of Finance,* Vol. 21 (September 1966), pp. 441–57.

Meltzer, Allan H. "The Demand for Money: The Evidence from the Time Series," *Journal of Political Economy,* Vol. 71 (June 1963), pp. 219–46.

Motley, Brian. "A Demand-for-Money Function for the Household Sector—Some Preliminary Findings," *Journal of Finance,* Vol. 22 (September 1967), pp. 405–18.

Smith, Paul E. "Money Supply and Demand: A Cobweb?" *International Economic Review,* Vol. 8 (February 1967), pp. 1–12.

Starleaf, Dennis R., and Richard Reimer. "The Keynesian Demand Function for Money: Some Statistical Tests," *Journal of Finance,* Vol. 22 (March 1967), pp. 71–76.

Stedry, Andrew C. "A Note on Interest Rates and the Demand for Money," *Review of Economics and Statistics,* Vol. 41 (August 1959), pp. 303–07.

Teigen, Ronald L. "Demand and Supply Functions for Money in the United States: Some Structural Estimates," *Econometrica,* Vol. 32 (October 1964), pp. 476–509.

Tobin, James. "Liquidity Preference and Monetary Policy," *Review of Economic Statistics,* Vol. 29 (May 1947), pp. 124–31.

_____. "Monetary Velocity and Monetary Policy: A Rejoinder," *Review of Economics and Statistics,* Vol. 30 (November 1948), pp. 314–17.

The following article reports empirical results showing no relationship between the demand for money and the rate of interest:

Friedman, Milton. "The Demand for Money: Some Theoretical and Empirical Results," *Journal of Political Economy,* Vol. 67 (June 1959), pp. 327–51.

index